PRAISE FOR BIO

I am a child and adult psychiatrist with thirty years of experience. Over the last four years during my training as a bioenergetic analyst, I have seen dramatic results with this form of therapy. I have seen transformations, growth, achievements of potential, people becoming more successful in their careers and personal lives, and people changing their careers successfully. I have seen amazing personal growth in terms of people becoming more connected to themselves and others, and I've seen people get better at self-regulation and gain a much greater capacity to handle stress and be able to enjoy life.

—Elias Sarkis, MD
Gainesville, FL

Bioenergetic therapy has been transformative for me. I am no longer trapped in my old patterns of behavior. I am more emotionally in tune with myself and therefore have more choice as to how to handle those emotions. As a result, I feel more settled and calm, my breath is fuller, my movements more fluid. A huge surprise for me has been the change in how I experience myself as a woman and as a sexually alive person. I highly recommend the bioenergetic method!

—Anne
St. Augustine, FL

In therapy, it's important to connect with and approach people as whole human beings in the context of their relationships and their work. Bioenergetic methods put people deeply and vitally in touch with who they are, so they can live life more authentically—and in a real and present way work through strong feelings and stuck patterns. Through the bioenergetic work, vibrant well-being can emerge, the ground of the self can be more directly experienced and expressed, relationships can become more deeply satisfying, and work can become more effective and fulfilling.

—Charles Martin, PhD, licensed psychologist
Gainesville, FL

As a therapist, utilizing bioenergetic therapy is highly effective in engaging a client at a much deeper level. Patterns are quickly identified, and the person is able to connect to the stuck emotions in a very real and present way. This allows for expression, release, freedom, and renewal—emotionally, physically, relationally, sexually, cognitively, spiritually. This is a powerful and dynamic tool for every therapist.

—Peggi S. Wegener, LMHC
Jacksonville, FL

My experience as a therapist and as a teacher in bioenergetics is based on personal experience and conceptual awareness that the body is the best path to higher levels of vitality and joy. The benefits of bioenergetics are physical, emotional, interpersonal, and a way to reach greater spiritual connection.

—Soledad Valenzuela, MA, Psych. Lic
Santiago, Chile

To improve your ability to watch and comment on life as it passes by, choose a talk-based therapy. To live your life in the driver's seat—feeling every twist and turn and becoming more skilled at steering and acceleration—choose bioenergetics.

—Jerry
Dallas, TX

Bioenergetic therapy improved my life in every possible sense. This amazing body psychotherapy helped me reconnect with my essence, helped me to honor and respect it, and gave me the tools to open myself to joy and pleasure. I now stay more in the present, live more fully, and allow myself to experience and trust my feelings. Bioenergetics opened the door to a new and better life for me.

—Elizabeth
Buenos Aires, Argentina

On my quest for self-improvement I found bioenergetic analysis. It quickly amazed and fascinated me. At first, I learned how to express my anger and sadness. Then I became aware of a wider range of emotions and started to understand myself even better. The bioenergetic method became my major tool for self-improvement, and I can't imagine my life without it.

—Szczepan
Warsaw, Poland

I have had a few regular talk therapists over the years. They were able to help me a little bit with my anxiety and depression. But nothing seemed to last. Finally, I found a wonderful bioenergetic therapist. I was able to get grounded, feel centered, and work through the root causes of my depression and overwhelming anxiety. It was a path to freedom and a more expressive and vibrant life. Thank you, bioenergetics, for your contribution to my happiness.

—Katherine
Denver, CO

In working with my clients, it is very clear how much bioenergetics helps them in their process of change. This is because bioenergetics enables individuals to work on mind and body levels simultaneously. By releasing tensions in their bodies, clients increase their level of energy and deepen their breath. Over time they begin to recognize and understand their emotions better. They learn how to express emotions fully, yet appropriately, which increases the quality of their communication and gives them a good foundation for better relationships. Bioenergetics provides clients the opportunity to see themselves for who they really are, to better understand their resources and limits, and to start to accept themselves more deeply. In the end, after a consistent effort and commitment to the process, they will begin to have access to deep joy and pleasure

—Grzegorz Byczek, certified bioenergetic therapist,
Warsaw, Poland

PRAISE FOR LEAH BENSON AND *EMOTIONAL UTOPIA*

I have known Leah Benson for several years and know clearly that her insights into human behavior are founded on principles well established in bioenergetics. However, the uniqueness of her approach constitutes a refreshing look at the method that opens new doors. To anyone wanting to improve, evolve, and achieve their goals, this work is worth serious consideration.

—Dr. Henri Marcoux, DC
Winnipeg, Canada

As a colleague of Leah Benson's, I've seen her in action as a therapist and facilitator, bringing her powerful blend of perception, compassion, and expertise to her analytic and energetic work with clients. She is a gifted and insightful professional who creates an environment where change can take place—and she is someone who practices what she preaches.

—Charles Martin, PhD, licensed psychologist
Gainesville, FL

Leah Benson challenges conventional psychoanalytic thinking. She understands that what most of us need is not a psychological assessment but rather a healthy human relationship. Leah is a talented therapist, but more importantly, she is a kindhearted human being. She taught me how to be compassionate toward myself by extending unconditional warmth to me first.

—Dane
Ontario, Canada

Being in the presence of Leah at work is to feel safe and trusting. She creates a safe space where our innermost pain, suffering, and fears can be expressed and contained. Leah reads body signals and expressions to understand information about the person. Then she combines this knowledge with psychoanalytic understanding of verbal expressions to make sense of the body's language. In the end, one finds grounding, a better sense of self, and more integration with mind, body, and soul.

—Mr. Bagua
Ft. Lauderdale, FL

When starting couples therapy with Leah, I was very skeptical at first upon hearing about bioenergetics. But when combined with the talking aspect, you discover (as a client) how interconnected your body and mind are—as one machine that is constantly trying to maintain harmony with itself. What I was most surprised at was the amount of energy the body stores from everyday events, especially trauma, that needs to be released to alleviate your own suffering. The power and methods of this approach accomplish that very effectively.

—Kevin
Tampa, FL

From my very first session with Leah, I knew that she was different—that the type of therapy (bioenergetic therapy) was different and that it might actually work. I have tried different types of therapy on and off through the years. I can say that I have made a considerable amount of forward progress since I started working with Leah and the method of therapy that she uses.

—Beatrice
Tampa, FL

I've only been working with Leah for a few months, and I've noticed that I've become much more present within myself. She has this way of making you feel comfortable even if you're uncomfortable with yourself. The bioenergetic method of therapy has helped with uncovering feelings and experiences I can't verbalize. Leah guides you throughout the process but never pushes beyond the point that you're uncomfortable. I'm finally starting to be okay with feeling, and it's all because of her.

—JJ
Tampa, FL

Leah's work with me was transformative. She really understood how my life worked (and didn't) and what mattered to me. She had the right mix of caring and "no B.S." that helped me uncover some of the painful blocks in my life keeping me from living happily and successfully. Through the analysis and energetic work, I felt freer and was able to find more effective and satisfying ways of being in my work, in my relationships, and with myself.

—Hans
Gainesville, FL

I know Leah as a well-grounded, compassionate, and skilled therapist as well as a warm-hearted and self-aware person with a healthy sense of humor. Leah's years of training and experience in psychoanalysis, along with a healthy dose of pure intuition, add to her bioenergetic sessions. She creates a safe space for clients to express and process locked-away feelings.

—Viviane Hens, LPC
Atlanta, GA

"Leah uses a diverse array of techniques that have really helped me. From traditional to bioenergetics--her methods are highly effective. Her ability to empathize and then integrate that into a mind opening experience is absolutely profound. She has literally changed my life to help get me back on the best path."

—Dave
Tampa, FL

"What I like about bioenergetic therapy is that I get results quickly and I typically feel better right after the session. It's powerful stuff, so having the right therapist is crucial. Leah Benson is just that professional. She has a strong psychoanalytic foundation and can navigate the intense and complicated emotions that arise quickly as a result of bioenergetic therapy. Over 30 years ago, I practiced bioenergetic therapy with a group that had little or no psychological training. The result for me was traumatic. The group did not have the skill to deal with the emotions that hard core bioenergetic therapy releases. And by "hard core" bioenergetic therapy, I mean that I was committed to positive change and took the exercises to heart. I put my "all" into the therapy. Leah Benson is a trusted professional psychoanalyst. She has made me feel very safe and has guided me through storms that previously consumed me. I have experienced very positive results from my work with Leah and I recommend her highly.

—Matthew
Tampa, FL

EMOTIONAL
UTOPIA

EMOTIONAL UTOPIA

STOP SEARCHING FOR HAPPINESS
AND START LIVING IT

LEAH BENSON

LMHC, EdM

Published by Advantage, Charleston, South Carolina.
Member of Advantage Media Group.

ADVANTAGE is a registered trademark and the Advantage colophon is a trademark of Advantage Media Group, Inc.

Printed in the United States of America.

ISBN: 978-1-59932-685-6
LCCN: 2016941954

Book design by Matthew Morse.

This publication is designed to provide accurate and authoritative information in regard to the subject matter covered. It is sold with the understanding that the publisher is not engaged in rendering legal, accounting, or other professional services. If legal advice or other expert assistance is required, the services of a competent professional person should be sought.

 Advantage Media Group is proud to be a part of the Tree Neutral® program. Tree Neutral offsets the number of trees consumed in the production and printing of this book by taking proactive steps such as planting trees in direct proportion to the number of trees used to print books. To learn more about Tree Neutral, please visit **www.treeneutral.com.**

Advantage Media Group is a publisher of business, self-improvement, and professional development books and online learning. We help entrepreneurs, business leaders, and professionals share their Stories, Passion, and Knowledge to help others Learn & Grow. Do you have a manuscript or book idea that you would like us to consider for publishing? Please visit **advantagefamily.com** or call **1.866.775.1696.**

For Claudette, who guided me to lasting happiness.

TABLE OF CONTENTS

FOREWORD

Your destiny is determined by how fully and deeply you *breathe.*

Humans are breathing machines. Take away our ability to breathe, and you take away our ability to live. Breath is life, and how you breathe has a tremendous impact on how you'll live.

Breathing is both a conscious and unconscious activity. On one hand we are consciously aware of our breathing when being suffocated or choking on something. On the other hand, we spend most of our day breathing with very little concern.

Breathing is a biomechanical mechanism, meaning that our body moves when we breathe. How our body moves is determined by factors including injury, poor posture, and muscular imbalances. Poor posture caused by muscular imbalances can occur both physically and psychologically.

Physical injuries, sedentary lifestyle, and ill health may clearly be seen as causes for poor posture and muscular imbalances. What is not as obvious is how our minds and emotions also create physical tensions and imbalances within the muscular system.

Our beliefs and our judgments have physical consequences. For example, we may remember a time when we were in the presence of someone who did us wrong. We may not have been aware of it, but our breathing frequency and depth was disturbed. All of this happens at an unconscious level, meaning that it is a habit.

One way to gain self-control is by first noticing the habit. By attuning ourselves to the sensations in our bodies, we become aware of when we are reacting out of habit. We might go further, though, and seek to confront the belief that is causing us to react in the first place.

This is where a good method for analysis becomes necessary. To explore the roots of the muscular holding patterns that impede deep, life-giving breath, we must explore the symbols, patterns, and experiences stored in the unconscious.

Leah Benson and I met at a bioenergetic analysis workshop in 2013.

Leah was a skilled psychotherapist looking for the missing piece to helping her clients. Having already become a master of the traditional psychoanalytic method, she is now paving the way for a new approach to psychoanalysis through bodily sensation, movement, and deep breathing.

Her method joins together the brilliant insights and life-affirming value of psychoanalysis with the practice of bioenergy expansion through deep breathing and movement.

Emotional utopia is our natural state and is felt when we breathe in a relaxed state.

Our body is relaxed because our mind is relaxed.

And our mind is relaxed because our body is relaxed.

We are alive and breathing.

—Elliott Hulse
Owner, Strength Camp

INTRODUCTION

Welcome to your first step toward emotional success. You want happiness, peace of mind, and enjoyable relationships, and I want you to have them. I want you to know that, yes, there is help for someone like you—someone strong, successful, and accomplished.

You're probably thinking, *There's nothing wrong with me. I don't really need help.* And you're right: there is nothing wrong with you. But maybe there's nothing that great, either. Maybe life is just okay or mediocre. You wonder why you're not happier.

You want something *more* or more meaningful out of life.

What if you were to feel really good more often, without having to be doing something to feel that way? If you're not emotionally satisfied, if you can't feel joy, or if you don't have good emotional connections with the intimate people in your life, there's definitely something wrong with *that*, and you know it.

Every day, I help people figure out what is keeping them from being happy. And every day, I help them develop internal tools to build the happiness they seek.

In this book you will learn, first and foremost, that you can be happy. You will learn about my proven method, bioenergetic psychoanalysis. You will learn why and how it works, and you will understand clearly how it can help you live the life you imagine for yourself.

The secret to happiness is being satisfied with who you are—deep down, in that private place, where you question yourself. Wouldn't you like to start doing the things you say you want to do? Or stop doing the things you don't want to do but keep doing anyway? Doesn't emotional satisfaction and lifelong peace of mind sound great?

After going through the method described in this book, you will feel satisfied with who you are, and you will be free from any invisible tethers holding you back from the emotional achievements noted above. Enjoyable intimate relationships, understanding and controlling any once-mysterious behaviors, and an overall, ongoing experience of satisfaction with life will all be yours.

How do I know? I know because I did it, and it completely changed my life. I was "perfectly normal." I was your basic "achiever" in an Ivy League master's degree program in psychology. I was moving forward with my life and had plenty of friends. It did not look as if there were anything "wrong" with me by any stretch of the imagination, and there was not, but . . .

It's kind of a truism that people go into psychology because they want to figure out their own stuff. I was no exception! I didn't have big problems, but I definitely had things to work on. My emotions would run really high or low. I would fall into funks for no apparent reason. The quality of my intimate relationships was "dramatic," to say the least. I was kind of a spaz. I definitely could not say I was happy, and I did not have peace of mind.

Exercise helped me handle my emotions and kept them from running very high and low. But it was not enough. In graduate school, after one of my classes stirred up a lot of feelings I did not know what to do with, I made the decision to get help for myself. I did not want to manage with exercise, alcohol, medication, or anything else. I wanted to *thrive*.

I started seeing a psychoanalyst twice a week, which quickly shifted to three times a week. I was like a fish in water, growing by leaps and bounds. I could not get enough of the stuff. All in all, I had ten years of analysis, ranging in frequency from once a month to four times a week. It was the most valuable investment of my life.

Ten years is a long time, and occasionally, I complained, "Why is this taking so long?" But it was worth it. When I finished, things were really good. I was emotionally satisfied, and I was happy with myself and my life. I was no longer plagued by bouts of misery or inexplicable periods of sluggishness. My relationships also felt really good. I did not waste time getting caught up in personal or interpersonal drama. All of this has remained, and since then, I have moved forward in life with a satisfaction that I know most people do not have—and may even envy.

As I worked with people in my own analytic therapy practice, I found that they often weren't experiencing their feelings in my office. Unfortunately, if you aren't able to *feel* your feelings and be real, you will never get the results you want. You are wasting your time on half-baked attempts.

Let's say you seek help because you want to enjoy the fruits of your labor, but you currently feel bored or even miserable. If you don't access the emotions behind these symptoms and the motivating beliefs they fuel, you will not change.

If your coping strategy is to completely avoid emotions, nothing you do in a talk-therapy or coaching setting is going to give you access to the feelings in your body. The power behind your negative beliefs will never be eliminated, and you will never see lasting results.

But there is good news. If you release the emotional power behind beliefs that fuel your symptomatic behavior, the behavior will be eliminated.

Since psychoanalysis works but takes a long time, I began to wonder how I could help people reach happiness and emotional satisfaction faster. I decided there had to be a better way. Feeling is in the body, so I wanted to get folks more connected to their bodies. I had to help them get out of their heads. It was a vague idea, but I knew it needed to happen. The body is the key.

Then, one day by random chance, I found myself listening to a lecture by the YouTube health and fitness celebrity Elliott Hulse. It was about deep breathing and called "Breathing into Your Balls." This really means breathing fully and relaxing your muscles all the way down into your pelvic floor as you inhale. The lecture was based on ideas of bioenergetic analysis, developed by Alexander Lowen, MD. The therapeutic method involves deliberately focusing on the body to access emotion. I was stunned. This was the answer I had been looking for.

It turned out there was a Society for Bioenergetic Analysis in Florida, not too far from where I lived. It offered a training program for therapists. I contacted the organization immediately. Within three weeks, I had an individual bioenergetic therapy session, and I was accepted into the program. A month later, I started training.

Incidentally, throughout the book, I will use the terms *bioenergetic analysis, bioenergetic therapy,* and *bioenergetics* interchangeably. They are the same thing. Dr. Lowen officially called it bioenergetic analysis, but he also referred to it as bioenergetic therapy and bioenergetics.

Before I went to that first individual bioenergetic therapy session, I really felt I was done with my own therapy. Overall, I was happy and often described myself as peaceful, despite the fact that I'm a pretty intense person. Going to the session was more of a novelty for me. But lo and behold, I discovered in that session, and the ones to follow, all kinds of emotions were still hiding in my body, fueling powerful unconscious beliefs. I became aware of many ways in which

I was, in fact, holding myself back from things that I wanted to do and had not been doing.

Since then, I have had many bioenergetic therapy sessions. I know bioenergetics works because it worked for me and has worked for my clients. It enables people to identify and access deep emotions that more conventional therapies are powerless to touch. I have gained a new insight and control over my life that has taken me to the next level. I incorporate bodywork into my practice as long as my clients are willing to try it, and I think they are ready for the intensity of the experience.

As I mentioned earlier, psychoanalysis changed my life, and subsequently, bioenergetic analysis has taken me to an even higher level of satisfaction. I am now a completely different person. I did not lose anything or become someone else, but I am "more": I am flexible, able to react and respond in ways that are appropriate to whatever situation is at hand. I'm not locked "in character," meaning that I don't do things because "that's the way I am." I have the energy to do what I need to do when I need to do it because I'm no longer bogged down with managing excess emotional energy that I was once unable to release. I feel joy easily. I have peace of mind, and I am happy.

Here's the thing: you are a capable, competent, successful person. You are accustomed to making things happen on your own. But in the area of emotional satisfaction, you are stuck. You may have used all the logic and rationality you could summon but have found that you still cannot make a problem go away, or maybe, you still cannot feel the joy and peace of mind you know exists and that you should have.

You may have tried exercise, yoga, massage, or escaping from your routine, but none of these brought lasting results. Did you try medication but didn't like it, or it didn't work? Maybe you gained insight or learned strategies from some other form of therapy but still didn't achieve the lasting outcome you'd hoped for. You want deeper answers and a better solution than you have been able to reach on your own. I bet you know from past experience that having insight into why you do things is not necessarily going to make them change.

If any of these descriptions apply to you, don't give up. You *can* be happy, emotionally satisfied, and free from the restraints that are holding you back from being your best self. The analytic method is powerful. It has made a huge difference in my life and in the lives of my clients. A few of their stories are included throughout this book. (Please note that individuals' names and identifying details have been significantly changed to protect their privacy.)

This is not a self-help book. Rather, it is a book to help you understand how committing to bioenergetic psychoanalysis will help you access unknown internal resources and, ultimately, the life you want. You will understand emotions much better, and you will be familiar with the unconscious. You will also understand bioenergetic bodywork and why intense bodywork is most effective (and safer) when practiced under the guidance of a psychotherapist.

That said, I've included some basic exercises you can do at home to give you an idea of the bodywork and its effects. I've also included a Notes and Resources section to help you find qualified professionals and additional information if you decide you would like to pursue this method further.

Quite simply, if I ask, "Are you emotionally satisfied? Do you have peace of mind?" and you cannot say yes, fully and whole-heartedly, then read on.

First, you'll learn what I mean by *happiness* and what you may be doing to keep yourself from experiencing it. You'll learn how psychotherapy (both talk-centered therapy and therapy that includes bodywork) operates. You will also see clearly how my method can put you in a position to say, "I am happy, I have peace of mind, and I am satisfied with myself and my life."

By the end of this book I hope you realize that emotional utopia is not a fantasy but, rather, the experience of life with an optimal balance of rich and varied emotions.

If you have never had therapy, it may seem mysterious and intrusive. Once you understand it, though, I believe you'll feel absolutely enthusiastic. You deserve to be happy.

Chapter 1

I'm Not Really Happy, but Isn't That Too Much to Ask?

Do you feel that something is "off" in your life? The joy is not there. Your relationships are not satisfying. You don't enjoy things as you used to. Perhaps you even feel you have it all . . . but you're not happy.

Maybe you've tried everything. Maybe you have a shelf of books that promised to help but didn't deliver. Satisfaction still eludes you. If that's the case, I've got good news. What you are looking for—call it happiness, emotional satisfaction, or peace of mind—is attainable.

To achieve it, you will have to get to know parts of yourself that you don't even know exist. It's hard to believe, I know, but there are parts of you that you don't know exist.

When I say "parts," what I mean is unconscious feelings and beliefs. So if that is not what you want to hear, you should stop reading now. Put down the book and keep searching. But if you can muster the courage to take a plunge into your unconscious and make peace with it, you will enjoy your life, and you will be happy.

The method I can guide you through, called bioenergetic psychoanalysis, will take you there.

FEELING YOUR WAY TO PEACE OF MIND

You may be thinking, *I don't enjoy my feelings, so why would feeling them make me feel better?* or *I want to be happy but I have all these responsibilities and challenges in my way.*

There is reason to persist. Read on.

First off, know that no matter how much success or wealth you have or how many difficult circumstances you face, these things do not control how happy you are. Happiness is not sunshine

HAPPINESS

1. Is not what is happening to you in any given moment

2. Is how you experience what is happening to you: your presence and acceptance in the moment without self-judgment

3. Depends on your ability to emotionally regulate; coping with what is happening, good or bad, is essential to whether you feel happiness or not

4. Requires finding the right balance of acceptance and regulation so you can feel the joys of life and handle the down times

and rainbows all the time. It is the peace of mind that comes with truly *feeling*, experiencing your emotions fully without self-judgment about them, *all the time.*

Happiness comes from the ability to calm down when you are upset and cheer up when you are down. That's called emotional regulation. It is having enough natural energy to get through the day without artificial stimulants. It is being able to fully feel life's joys and sorrows without being overwhelmed or crushed by them.

In other words, happiness is not always about feeling "happy." It is more. It is the ability to experience good feelings and not be controlled by bad ones.

Are you thinking you don't have a lot of extra time and wondering if this will take years and years of sitting around and discussing your problems? That is a legitimate concern. I don't promise anyone a miraculous quick fix. Gaining skills to achieve the successful balance that defines emotional utopia takes time. Do you want to invest in a lifelong solution or temporary relief?

Ask yourself what you are willing to commit to in order to be emotionally satisfied for the rest of your life.

How Bioenergetic Psychoanalysis Works

In the chapters that follow, I will explain exactly what happens in bioenergetic psychoanalysis and how it can help you find happiness. First, you will learn about traditional talk therapy, specifically, *psychoanalysis*. After that, I will explain how bioenergetics speeds up the process and, in most cases, helps you find success you would never achieve with talk therapy.

Psychotherapy in the psychoanalytic tradition (which you'll learn more about in chapter 3) uses your relationship and conversations with a therapist to discover three things:

- your unconscious motivations or beliefs
- how the unconscious motivations or beliefs are simultaneously affecting and fueled by your emotions
- how to use this knowledge to lead a happier life

A simplified version of the method looks like this: The therapist notices and reflects to you the ways you react to the process of therapy and to the therapist. Then you and the therapist analyze that information in the context of your life.

This process illuminates much about your life patterns. It's not something you can do on your own. Analyzing a relationship pattern without input from both parties leaves too many blind spots.

Often, what is revealed feels shameful or embarrassing. Past learning through prior relationships with important people has taught you to feel that way. You might even have no conscious awareness of the feelings as they are happening because that is the way you have learned to manage shameful or embarrassing feelings. (This is why people don't like to be "analyzed.")

After going through repeated experiences of this kind with your therapist, you develop new beliefs about yourself and the feelings you revealed and acknowledged. You are no longer ashamed or embarrassed about them, because someone important in your life has accepted you even though you revealed them.[1] This is healing.

Bioenergetic analysis has the same goals as talk therapy: to help you discover your unconscious motivations or beliefs, to understand how they simultaneously affect and are fueled by your emotions, and to allow you to use this knowledge to lead a happier life. It is based on the following premise backed by decades of research in neuroscience, as we'll discuss in chapter 6.

What goes on in your mind that keeps you from being happy is manifested in your body and can therefore be addressed by working through the body.

To reach unconscious issues, instead of relying on analysis of what happens in your relationships, bioenergetic analysis relies on analyzing and then working with your body to uncover the drivers of your behavior. This pathway to discovery works faster than traditional psychotherapy, and for some people, it works much better.

---

[1] This means the therapist has to be important and/or significant. It is why you want to feel good about whomever you choose as your therapist, right from the beginning.

Combine the analysis of what happens in your relationships with the bodywork of bioenergetic analysis, and you have bioenergetic psychoanalysis.

Both bioenergetics and psychoanalysis have a common pitfall: clients sometimes leave prematurely. The speed at which feelings can be uncovered through bodywork and the fact that "unacceptable" thoughts or feelings arise can both feel threatening. Clients may feel ill-equipped to deal with the intensity of their emotions and unwilling to share with the therapist, with whom they have not developed a strong enough bond or enough trust to help them handle the experience.

If this happens to you, don't quit. Stick with the process, and talk through the rough spots with your therapist. Without doing so, you will shortchange yourself. Navigating difficulties face-to-face is a critical component of the method that you must experience to achieve lasting results.

MIND TRICKS AND RATIONALIZATIONS

It helps to know that on your way to achieving happiness, you will be your own worst enemy. We all play mind tricks on ourselves, and many of our "problems" are symptoms of those tricky patterns of thought.

We talk ourselves out of feelings that we have—or do not want to have—because they might hurt someone else's feelings. We rationalize. When we are angry with someone we like, we may tell ourselves, *I don't need to be angry about this. Shit happens.* Talking ourselves out of feelings does not lead to feeling better, though. It leads to feeling stuck or feeling nothing at all. We may go even further in rationalizing: *I have everything I want. I don't need to feel happy—or anything, really.*

We also use mind tricks and rationalizations in thinking about relationships. A client once said to me, "Maybe I don't need to have a close relationship with anyone. Maybe I'm not the kind of person who wants to be in a relationship, and I need to be alone."

The truth is we are wired to be in relationships. We are social beings, and our brain is a social organ. Anything else we tell ourselves is a trick to avoid feelings that we would have to address in order to be in a satisfying, long-term relationship.

Rationalizations are a common strategy that successful people use to get and stay successful. They help us live in society and face circumstances. But we run into problems when we believe we're never supposed to let out "unacceptable" feelings.

WHEN THERAPY IS RELEVANT

If you say any of the following things to yourself, therapy—and bioenergetic psychoanalysis in particular—can help:

- I have a great life! I'm successful, I'm healthy, I work out, I'm in control. But I'm not *happy*.
- Something is missing in my life. I'm not really unhappy, but things don't excite me.
- I'm going through the motions every day.
- My spouse loves me, my kids behave, and I have a successful career. I don't know what my problem is, but I don't feel good.
- I feel stuck.
- I feel empty, kind of numb.
- I feel guilty about everything.
- I lash out at people when I don't want to.
- I hate my body.
- I feel too much . . . too intensely.
- I get sick a lot.
- I have no self-confidence.
- My sex life is bad.
- I worry obsessively.
- It seems as if I'm always getting headaches or stomachaches.
- Exercise is great, but I don't stick with it, and I go back to my old ways.
- I wish I weren't such a perfectionist.
- I don't feel good about life.

This can, ultimately, lead to believing that we don't even have those feelings. Here's how it works.

When you were young you were probably taught, as most of us were, that there was no time or place to let out feelings such as anger, fear, sadness, weakness, or longing. As an infant, you had no filter on emotional responses to the feelings in your body or to external stimuli. Your feelings flowed until you experienced relief.

From as early as four months of age,[2] you received messages about the acceptability of your emotions. Your caregiver might have reacted to emotional displays by ignoring them, ridiculing or threatening you, or manipulating you into stopping them. To develop emotional control, you contracted your muscles and held your body stiff. These contractions might have been massive or incredibly subtle. Over time, the emotion-controlling contractions became automatic, and you became skilled at hiding "unacceptable" feelings.

You were unaware this was happening. But the process is real and is the basis of much of your unconscious mind.

For most people, the message to contain "unacceptable" emotions was frequent and unmistakable. You learned that unless you felt justified, there was no reason to express certain feelings. You gradually convinced yourself that you didn't have them. This inevitably resulted in the holding back of a ton of feeling, similar to a flooding lake behind a dam. That's when disaster can strike.

Surely you can remember times when you blew up at someone for no reason. It was not about the other person, really. It was about an old hurt from long ago that you had no consciousness of at the time of the explosion. The feelings came out, and you had no idea why.

---

[2] Beatrice Beebe et al., "The Origins of 12-Month Attachment: A Microanalysis of 4-Month Mother-Infant Interaction," *Attachment & Human Development* 12, no. 1–2 (Jan. 2010): 3–141, doi:10.1080/14616730903338985.

WHY DO ALL THAT WORK?

Only when you focus on becoming aware of unconscious motivations for your behavior can you make mindful choices to act differently. Unfortunately, knowledge of the experiences that are motivating your current behavior is often not enough to help you change your behavior.

In bioenergetic psychoanalysis, you will actually go through the emotions connected with old experiences that you have been holding in your body for all these years. That will wash them out of you for good. Their power to energize negative beliefs and behaviors that undermine you will be gone.

> ## BIOENERGETIC PSYCHOANALYSIS IN A NUTSHELL
>
> - Bioenergetic psychoanalysis will move you toward the achievement of happiness by helping you reveal unconscious beliefs, dislodge stuck emotions, and integrate that information and experience into your conscious awareness and "story" of your life.
>
> - Your emotions may be eluding you, but they can be found in the chronic tensions of your muscles
>
> - Understanding of the source of your pain or numbness comes through experiencing the physical sensation of emotion under the guidance of a trained practitioner.
>
> - The body hides these clues to your emotions, but bodywork can help you quickly become aware of your body and make conscious the feelings that were once unconscious.
>
> - To achieve *lasting* happiness and peace of mind, it's crucial to combine bioenergetic analysis with psychoanalysis.

Why do this—*repeatedly*—to yourself? Because if you want to change your life, you must change the structured patterns in your body and mind.

You have to unlearn what you learned the first time about managing feelings. You must overwrite your old, ineffective, automatic system of managing them with a new one. And you must practice a new way of experiencing and expressing your feelings so that this new way becomes your unconscious, or automatic, way.

> ## *When you stop wasting energy on old, ineffective ways of living, you will discover untapped resources within you.*

If you still think that happiness sounds like a lot to ask for, let me reassure you that it is a reasonable goal. I'll let you in on the secrets—of yourself and of happiness—as we go along. You will soon realize there is no real secret to it. It takes some work and some guidance, but emotional satisfaction and peace of mind can be yours.

CHAPTER 2

What Does Happiness Feel Like?

We've defined happiness as the peace of mind that comes with being able to acknowledge and accept all your feelings all the time, having enough natural energy to get through the day, and being able to feel both the ups and the downs of life without being overwhelmed or crushed by them.

But what does happiness really *feel* like?

That depends on you and what excites you or makes you mad, sad, or glad. It might feel like the thrill of victory. It might feel like the first cool breeze of autumn blowing across your skin or the taste of your favorite dessert. It can feel like the first time you fell in love or the sweet feeling of looking at your new baby.

Since our lives are filled not with only positive experiences but a range of good and bad, it can also feel like the welling up of anger at an injustice you realize has occurred to you or someone you love. It can feel like the sadness you experience at the passing of a loved one or the loss of something important to you.

Happiness feels like the satisfaction of having the ability and strength to experience a whole range of emotions as they move through you, informing you about what's happening inside you and around you, without judgment of yourself for having them.

Contentment versus Happiness

Some people call this state *contentment* rather than *happiness*. I use the word *joy* to describe the *happy* state you may be thinking about, and I use the word *happiness* to describe what many people call *contentment*. You can use the words as you like, but remember that when I say happy, I'm not thinking of a passing emotion. I'm thinking of the long-term nature of contentment. I mean an overall sense of emotional satisfaction or peace of mind.

Joy, the elevated, positive experience of emotion, like anger or sadness, is a specific reaction. Joy, anger, and sadness are not ongoing states. Happiness, then, is when your mind agrees to and accepts specific emotional reactions in your body. Happy people do not suppress emotion by controlling it with their minds and tension in their bodies. They acknowledge, experience, and accept it consciously.

Feeling is not a bad thing, but being *overwhelmed* by, or experiencing shame about it, is. Therapy will broaden and deepen your capacity to consciously tolerate, contain, and release emotion. This is the foundation for happiness and the balanced state of emotional utopia.

When you finish therapy, you will *know* that emotions pass. You won't be joyful 100 percent of the time, but life will feel good unless something distinctly bad is happening at the moment.

You will be able to enjoy the simple things in life and feel joyfulness in any given moment. For example, you might notice light coming through a leaf after the rain and feel a sense of joy and connectedness to the world in that moment. You might notice the sunshine filtering through your sweetheart's hair and how that makes you feel. You will be able to share this feeling with her and feel her appreciating that you noticed it, which then allows the two of you to feel connected.

Small, emotionally satisfying moments such as these will become commonplace in your life.

GETTING UNLOCKED

When you can truly let your emotions move through you, *anything* can feel good. In contrast, if you chronically tense your body to block "unacceptable" feelings, you won't, as I've said, feel the simple joys in life, either.

For instance, say you're picking blueberries. You might feel great—content to enjoy the sun on your skin, your emotional connection to others picking blueberries with you, and the smells of nature. But if you're not in touch with your feelings, then you're out there in the sun picking blueberries, and it's your next activity for the day. You are like a drone. There's no feeling in it; you're just doing.

Many people whose feelings are locked up in this way are sensations seekers. In order to feel—and I mean in order to feel anything at all—sensation seekers constantly put themselves into extreme situations and sometimes dangerous places. Those situations might involve sex, drugs, extreme sports or careers, repeated combat situations, or any other physically stressful scenario.

To feel anything, your body has to *move* in some way, even if it's only at a very subtle level. If there is no movement, there is no feeling.

Say you're sitting and watching your child learn a new skill, and you're feeling joy. What movement is involved there? It's one that comes from your heart as you breathe freely, a feeling in your chest.

When your heart fills up with gladness, it is literally a feeling in your chest and in your heart. It's more than a metaphor.

In contrast, say you tend to hold your chest muscles very tight. The movement in your chest is so restricted by this chronic contraction of your muscles that it's not possible to feel anything there. You can feel no joy.

Being able to feel joy at the simplest things or to feel good in any plain old moment does not depend on your situation in life, be it financial status, job, or family. It's not about external circumstances or outward success. It's about what's going on inside.

No matter who or where you are, no matter what your outward circumstances may be, you can feel deep joy and emotional satisfaction when you are fully integrated with all of your feelings. A slogan I saw once said it best: "Happiness: it's an inside job."

What's Holding You Back?

Would you consider not brushing your teeth most days? Of course not, because you are a self-respecting, successful person. As a child, you were taught grooming methods for getting rid of the build-up of residue from daily life. Guess what? You have psychological build-up as well.

Parts of you that you are unaware of are influencing you in ways you don't know about. They diminish your effectiveness, your joy, and your spontaneity. They keep your relationships from being as satisfying as they could be.

Through the skills and experience you gain in analysis, you will be able to release that build-up. Hidden emotions that fuel hidden beliefs from childhood won't be holding you back from your happiest life.

You may think, *But I don't care about my childhood feelings! I'm an adult now.*

Here's the deal: childhood beliefs and feelings are important. You have to be conscious of them and experience them in the present. This has to happen in the context of a coherent story of your past. Only then will you achieve the peaceful, satisfying emotional state you're looking for.

Your thoughts and memories must be integrated with your feelings to achieve deep, lasting results. When this happens you will feel good in ways you never imagined possible. But to get there, you must revisit your childhood

For example, the experience that led me to start writing this book illustrates how feeling an emotion, as well as understanding its history and how it fuels our beliefs, can unlock our potential and be life-changing.

Like many of us, I have had a tendency to hold myself back from certain things. I was not even really aware I was doing it. I wanted to write my blog more frequently, and I'd been thinking about writing a book. Overall, I was happy and I was enjoying life, but I was not taking much initiative toward those goals—until the moment of the following story.

There I was, having a simple conversation that triggered a memory followed by a freight train of emotion.

Suddenly, I'm in first grade, the only kid wearing a faded uniform in my parochial school class.

I'm desperate to not be the only kid with a faded uniform. I hate feeling different. I feel *less* than the other kids. I want to have a uniform like everyone else's. I had begged my parents for a bright, new uniform, but they could not afford it. So I believe I'm not as good as all the other kids. I don't deserve to have what they have.

At the time I had this memory I was talking with someone who understood bioenergetics, and I was in an appropriate place to do it, so I burst into tears right then and there.

I allowed myself to be the six-year-old who was devastated rather than blocking the emotion with rationalizations and understanding my parents' financial reality. I let myself sob. And sob and sob.

This connected me to that emotional experience and my unconscious belief that I'm not as good as others or I don't deserve what I want.

Right then, I learned the secret that was holding me back from taking the steps to move myself toward what I wanted. I integrated it with an emotional experience that I discharged. Quite suddenly, I was no longer motivated by the

NINE SIGNS OF A HEALTHY MIND

If you are interested in pursuing greater happiness, take this quiz to see where you might be able to make improvements.

Brain research says that if you have the following nine attributes, you have a healthy mind. How many do you have?

- **Happiness:** *Can you feel joy in the simple experiences in your life?* Happiness is not a momentary response to a particular situation in your life; it is a general state of being. Some might call it peace of mind, contentment, or a sense of well-being. If you do not have an overall feeling of happiness about yourself and your life, despite whatever ups and downs your day-to-day life might bring you, you are missing a piece of the mental-health puzzle.

- **Flexibility:** *Do things have to be "just so" for you to be happy, or can you be flexible as circumstances, both major and minor, in your life change?* Being flexible means that you can adjust to your current circumstances without suffering too much depression, anxiety, or loss of focus on your goals and relationships.

- **Emotional regulation:** *Can you get yourself revved up to face life when you need to? Does it take you a long time to calm down* when angry or fearful feelings have overwhelmed you? Do you have knee-jerk reactions? The strength to push through the down times and the ability to turn down the burner on overarousal are functions of a healthy mind. When your skills in these areas are suffering, you know that your mental health could use some TLC.

- **Good relationships:** *Do you feel totally autonomous and at the same time completely connected to the most important people in your life?* If not, you have some work to do. The quality of your relationships is one of the biggest indicators of your overall mental health. Good relationships, both intimate and superficial ones, are characterized by kindness, compassion, and empathy.

- **Wisdom:** *Do you use experience, knowledge, and good judgment to drive the decisions you make and the actions you take in your life?* If not, this aspect of mental health eludes you. Sound decision making and the ability to foresee potential outcomes of the actions you take requires an integration of parts of your brain that only sound mental health allows.

- **Compassion:** *Can you feel the emotions of others? Do you show kindness, care, and a willingness to help relieve others of their suffering when it makes sense to do so?* We are social animals, and our ability to experience the

six-year-old inside me who believed she could not have and did not "deserve" to have what she wanted. I was free.

Since that moment, I have had no problem doing anything that I need to do in order to move myself toward what I want. I knocked out the blogs and wrote this book!

It was not simply gaining insight that allowed me to move forward. I'd actually had that memory previously. It was not new information. What I learned at that moment was that it was affecting me in the present. I'm a rational adult. I know I can give myself what I want and do the things I need to do to make things happen. Much to my surprise, though, the six-year-old belief was still motivating me to inaction.

We tell ourselves rational things all the time,

which often only helps superficially and temporarily. I still looked at Facebook instead of writing my blog entries, and I sat in front of the TV instead of writing this book. I would tell myself that maybe I was not really interested in that goal, or maybe I was a lazy person. The truth was something more.

The *emotional experience* of how painful it was to feel like that little girl is what made me truly aware for the first time of the existence and power of my childhood belief. I was living as if I were not deserving. And until that moment, I was completely unaware of the emotional power driving my lack of motivation.

I finally understood my failure to take active steps toward what I wanted, and then I was free of it.

emotions of others and respond with kindness, care, and a willingness to help is fundamental. If you do not possess this quality, it may be an indication that you are missing something in the healthy-mind department.

- **Morality:** *Do you have the capacity to think of the larger good and act in a prosocial way, even when you are alone?* Our social nature requires that we act in ways that benefit not only ourselves but our group as well. Antisocial and amoral behaviors are clear indicators of poor mental health.

- **A sense of meaning:** *Can you tell a coherent story of your life? Do you feel connected to something larger than yourself?* Being able to make sense of your life by telling your story and experiencing the feeling of being connected to something larger than yourself are indicators of healthy mental functioning.

- **Intuition:** *Are you aware of the information coming from your heart and your gut?* If not, your mental health is suffering. Believe it or not, a vital component of mental health is a connection to the neural networks of your heart and your intestines. If these connections are impaired or missing, you have some work to do.

If you answered no to a lot of these questions, you may have more pain in your past than you think. You could benefit from doing *any* kind of therapy. If there are only a few areas in which you answered negatively but you still feel that contentment and happiness elude you, then the bioenergetic psychoanalysis method is definitely for you. Your life will become more satisfying when you commit to it.

Consciously acknowledging and feeling the emotion of an old experience and connecting it to the story revealed the reality of the belief and removed its power.

Children make sense of everything that happens to them and around them as if it has something to do with them. They interpret events as if they are the center of the world. It's the only way they can make sense of things with their immature minds.

They *unconsciously* take that understanding to adulthood and act accordingly, as I had done.

Through this emotional experience in the presence of someone who was understanding, coupled with rational exploration, my behavior changed almost automatically. All three of these pieces are necessary for you to move forward and achieve happiness. Therapy provides all three.

In therapy, you have a private place to explore things about yourself that you are unaware of, that are holding you back, and that will inevitably change with enough repetition of new patterns.

Bioenergetic psychoanalysis supplies the relationship that is a critical component necessary for you to experience lasting change and growth. The next chapter will break down the basics of psychotherapy and how it can be helpful to you.

CHAPTER 3

How Does Psychotherapy Work?

Sometimes, when I say I'm a psychotherapist, a conversation stops in its tracks. Suddenly, drinks need refreshing. I get it. You don't need psychotherapy. It might be the last thing you'd be caught doing. No need to talk any further.

Maybe you are familiar with therapy from TV, movies, or reading. If so, toss that vision in the garbage. Psychotherapy is not like what you see in print or onscreen. Honestly, I have yet to see a show that does it justice.

Psychotherapy is a blanket term. It encompasses a huge number of methods. In fact, any method that involves at least two people and the goal of helping one of them with behaviors, thinking patterns, and/or emotions is psychotherapy. No matter what else you call it. Psychotherapy includes but is not limited to:

- psychoanalysis
- bioenergetic analysis
- cognitive behavioral therapies
- existential/humanistic therapies
- neurolinguistic processing/ hypnosis
- coaching (life or executive)

In this chapter I'll explain psychoanalysis, which is the foundation of the way I do psychotherapy. In the next chapter I'll explain bioenergetic analysis and how it differs from psychoanalysis. Along the way, I'll talk about my method for lasting results, which is a combination of the two and is called bioenergetic psychoanalysis.

It's a Relationship

All the reasons you might go to psychotherapy boil down to one fact: your brain is stuck in particular firing patterns that do not serve you well, and you can't change them on your own. It's that simple.

We'll talk about the science behind these brain patterns, or pathways, in chapter 6.

What you need to know for now is that your unconscious beliefs, feelings, and behaviors are manifestations of those unhelpful firing patterns. When they become conscious, you can change them through the willful repetition of different behaviors.

Unfortunately, the most difficult behaviors to change are motivated by beliefs you have not uncovered or beliefs you have not integrated with the feelings fueling them. Thus, they motivate your behavior no matter how strong your will.

There is an added complication. Most of your troublesome beliefs (brain firing patterns) were originally created in relationship to an authority with whom you were stuck and on whom you were emotionally dependent.

To change them requires comparable circumstances.

You, a fully functional, autonomous adult, must put yourself in a relationship with someone to whom you give authority over your emotional life—and with whom you are stuck. You must recreate as closely as possible the original circumstances in which the brain pathways that do not serve you well were created.

To change your brain's firing patterns, you must go through repeated experiences that build new brain pathways to override your old ones. In other words, you must do something different from anything you have ever done before, over and over again.

Luckily for you, the therapy relationship is unlike anything you have ever done (at least therapy with me is). In the process, those rascally brain firing patterns that keep you from achieving your goal of happiness will change.

You might wonder why you can't do it on your own. It's because, as I mentioned, those now-unhelpful firing patterns were created in a relationship. Conversely, they can only be changed in a relationship.

You can do a lot on your own to regulate your emotions, modify your behavior, and come to understand yourself by reflecting on experiences that you've had. However, changing how you unconsciously react in a relationship has to occur in the context of a relationship.

Therapy is the only relationship designed for that purpose.

But Why Would I Go to Therapy? I'm Not Crazy!

The stigma of psychotherapy is a holdover from the early days of the practice, during the time of Sigmund Freud.

Many of the people who consulted Dr. Freud were women with symptoms of hysteria. They were passing out and had numbness or paralysis. They had false pregnancies and any number of other *conversion* symptoms, meaning that their psychological issues were converted into, or manifested by, physical symptoms. There were definitely things "wrong" with them. Terrible things had happened to them, and they were having drastic reactions. They could not function in day-to-day life.

The tradition of associating therapy with this type of person has continued through time. Unfortunately, even today, there are also psychiatric "bibles" that continue to apply negative labels to symptoms, describing them as things that are "wrong" with people.

So if I were to say, "Go to therapy; it will help you," you'd look at me as if I were nuts, or you'd change the subject. If nothing terrible has happened to you, you had a decent childhood, your parents took good care of you, and you are a productive, functioning member of society, *of course*, you don't need therapy.

I agree, you don't *need* it. But are you happy? Do you have peace of mind? Does contentment last when you find it? And what about your intimate relationships: are they satisfying? If you picked up this book, my bet is you are looking for something more out of life. Psychotherapy, the way I do it, will help you get it. If you decide to try it, despite any turmoil over the idea, here's what we're going to do.

We're going to uncover, understand, and work through unconscious feelings and beliefs that are the basis of your unhappiness. That means you will experience, in "the now," emotions that were present at the time when a belief was created. Then the stories of your life and your emotions can be integrated. *Integration* is health, which, for you, means "peace of mind."

Your unconscious beliefs will no longer have the emotional power they need to motivate your actions, so you will feel different, and you will act differently. Remember my story about integrating my feelings with the belief that was holding me back from writing this book?

Over time, you won't need me to help you do this. You will be able to do it on your own.

For the rest of your life, you will have a set of keys that unlock the doors to emotional satisfaction and personal motivation.

ISN'T THERE AN EASIER PATH?

I know you want to move forward, to feel joy, and to be happy. The idea of feeling pain and old feelings seems stupid, I agree. If there were another answer, I would have done it myself, I promise you.

The only healthy and long-lasting way to the pleasure, happiness, and emotional satisfaction you want is through gaining the strength and skills to handle your feelings in a new way. Actually, you won't be handling your feelings at all, because you won't need to handle them. They will simply exist.

When you have spent most of your life getting rid of certain emotions through the use of self-talk, willpower, and chronic muscular contractions, you are probably convinced that you don't have certain feelings. The mind's tricks and rationalizations we talked about in the last chapter are part of the reason you are a successful, socially acceptable person. Unfortunately, they are also holding you back from being the best version of yourself that you can be.

If too much feeling is your problem, then strategies such as mindfulness and breathing techniques to manage your feelings and problematic behaviors have probably been helpful. You may have read self-help books or Googled ways to manage this or that emotional state. Techniques are definitely important for use in temporary situations. Sometimes, their benefits even last a while, but ultimately, they are doomed to fail. It's not that you aren't trying hard enough. Handling your feelings is not a matter of willpower. Willpower cannot overcome your unconscious mind indefinitely.

No matter what tricks you are using to avoid knowledge of certain feelings in consciousness, rest assured your body is still containing them, and the beliefs they fuel are causing you to act in ways that you cannot control. This has been happening all your life, but you don't see it. You can't, because that's what *unconscious* means. But they affect so much about you: how you hold your body, the way you walk, the way you stand, and even the way you interact with people.

I was talking with a friend who hunches her back very markedly. She had seen a photo of herself and was horrified by how hunched-over she looked. She asked me, "Do I do this all the time?" I answered gently, "Yes, you do it all the time, and there are times that are worse than others."

A hunched back is often the bodily representation of aggression that is not being acknowledged. My friend thought of herself as non-confrontational, but her aggression came out in her actions as passive aggressiveness. Other people often noticed it.

She did not express aggression on a conscious level, but unconsciously, she would do things such as repeatedly showing up late for meetings or losing her keys and standing someone up for a dinner date if that person had recently argued with her. She tried controlling her aggressive feelings with her mind, but her body and her indirect actions revealed them. She was shocked when I pointed this out to her.

Another example of an "unacceptable" feeling we try to avoid is longing. Nobody wants to admit to longing—wanting to be more special, feel more cared for, or have more—but we often feel it.

Jealousy and envy are borne of old experiences of not feeling very special or not getting as much of something as we wanted. Those old experiences, when unexamined and unintegrated into consciousness, fuel current-day adult wishes for more: you can't get enough; you're never satisfied.

It's impossible to suppress this longing if, at one time, you did not get "enough."

> If you want to be able to stop doing what you say you want to stop doing, start doing what you say you want to start doing, and feel overall happiness and peace of mind in your life, you will have to access old beliefs and dissipate the feelings associated with them that you have been holding in your body all your life. You will also have to overwrite an old, ineffective, automated system of managing feelings with a new one and practice it so that it becomes your automatic way. When this happens, you will have the life you want.

Before you say, "Not me," remember all this is going on at an unconscious level. You have no idea if or when it's happening until later, when things fall apart or hit the fan. People inadvertently create situations that force others to give them more.

People can go as far as becoming physically ill in order to receive the attention they needed "back when" and continue to long for. If that's not something you do, don't get too smug. You do *something* to indirectly meet your unconscious needs. We all do.

Numbing yourself—not feeling at all—to get rid of feelings won't work either. You won't feel anything bad, but you won't feel anything good. You will have no joy in your life.

Sensation is sensation. You cannot discriminate and choose to feel only good stuff. To be more sensitive to pleasure, you must be more sensitive to pain. And it's *old* unconscious pain that makes for most difficulties in adulthood.

WHAT TO EXPECT IN THE THERAPY RELATIONSHIP

Before I break down the nuts and bolts of how a therapy relationship works, I have to tell you there is a big difference between therapy for temporary relief/support and therapy for lifelong happiness. As a therapist, I'm happy to help you with either goal. You have to decide which one is for you.

Therapy for temporary relief and support comes in many forms.

It can be very short term, consisting of just a few sessions. It can happen more regularly, once a week or once every other week for six months to two years or longer. It might be intermittent—two or three times a year for a session or two, or once a month for many years. It might even be, for a short time, face-to-face, and then continue with intermittent

THERAPY: THE WEIRDEST *REAL* RELATIONSHIP YOU WILL EVER HAVE

The client-therapist relationship is an odd one. Many people think it will be the kind of relationship in which I'm the teacher, you're the student, and I'm teaching you things that you are going to be able to take away and use in your life. That is not what's happening. What is happening is that in this relationship, unlike what happens in others, we are deliberately using the relationship to change you. That's part of what makes it weird.

I can't tell you how many times I've heard people say that a therapy relationship is not a real relationship. To be honest, during a large part of my own therapy, I thought the same thing. I believed my therapist's reactions to me couldn't possibly be real, because I paid her to be nice to me. She wouldn't react to me so kindly in a real relationship, right?

Wrong! First, you do not pay a therapist to be nice to you. You pay her to provide her professional services, which include not being fake. Second, it's a relationship with different boundaries and expectations from those of any other, but that does not mean it's not real.

In every other intimate relationship, two people engage with each other under the assumption that their emotional needs will be met, even if only partially, by the other person.

In my relationship with you, as your therapist, the only thing I get to expect from you is the fee. I may end up feeling satisfied that I have helped you, but even that is not a guarantee, and it is not an expectation that I can fairly put on you. You do not have to be helped to satisfy me. That is what I want. That *would* satisfy me. But the whole relationship is about my setting aside my needs in order to help you.

If, as your therapist, I do not experience, acknowledge, and use my real reactions to you, I am not doing my job. Using my authentic reactions to help you is a huge part of my professional service.

Sharing my reactions with you in a kind way is another part of it. As I mentioned, unlike other relationships, the therapy relationship is deliberately one-sided. The whole relationship is about meeting your needs.

I must constantly monitor myself and question whether what I am doing is about meeting my needs or about helping you get yours met, within the boundaries set by the therapy relationship.

phone sessions. Some people only want phone, video, or even e-mail sessions.

Whatever the flavor, therapy sessions all start out the same.

First, as in any relationship, we will get to know each other. It will be pretty one-sided. You get to know me by the things you can see about me, the very few questions I will answer about myself, and the way you feel when you're with me.

In contrast, you will tell me everything you can think of that you believe is relevant about the problem you came for. You will tell me all the ways you have tried to solve that problem, what has worked, and what has not. You might tell me a little about your history and the important people in your life. We might talk about strategies I think could help bring you relief, or not,

depending on your interest in advice from me.

You will express yourself verbally and sometimes emotionally, and I will be an empathetic listener who sees you from an outside perspective and offers insight from that perspective. When you have gotten the relief you want, you will quit. If you need more support or relief later, you might come back. If you have an unresolved issue with me that we never talked about, you might go talk to someone else.

> It can be tricky because, like you, I am a real person with unconscious motivations. If things start going wrong, I have to determine if my behaviors might be affecting you, bring that to my conscious awareness, and fix it. This is one of the most difficult and most important skills of a therapist.
>
> If you ever find that you feel weird with your therapist and feel even worse after you bring the issue up to your therapist, something is very wrong. Keep pushing the issue, or find another therapist.
>
> Your relationship with your therapist is a real relationship, all right. But it feels weird because it's all about you. And that's uncomfortable.

Therapy leading to lifelong happiness begins in much the same way as therapy for temporary relief and support, but then it becomes very different. It has its rules. You come several times a week. You make a commitment—whatever it will take to keep you from walking away—so that, in essence, you are stuck in the process.

The commitment is necessary because you will start to feel, and fight, an emotional dependence on the support and positive attention you are experiencing. That might sound crazy, but a period of emotional dependence is a crucial part of the path to happiness. If therapy does not become an important part of your emotional life, my ability to influence positive changes in your brain is diminished or nonexistent. (Chapter 6 will explain why in more depth.) The longer it takes you to feel emotional dependence and to admit it, the longer the process will take. You will fight it with any means necessary, often including "needing" to leave therapy, usually with a very legitimate reason.

You will be expected to talk about anything and everything that comes to mind, including things you think about me and the process of therapy. When you find you don't want to say certain things because it's uncomfortable, you will be expected to discuss your discomfort. You will probably struggle with trusting me and trusting the process.

As the old-time psychoanalysts would say, you need "frequency and duration" to get lasting results. You have to commit to staying, no matter how difficult the journey becomes. You also have to believe in your therapist's authority; you have to know, like, and deeply trust her. This takes time because, at a fundamental level, you will resist it, having been disappointed and hurt by people you have entrusted your emotions to in the past.

If you like and trust someone, then you are vulnerable to the same kind of rejection for "unacceptable" emotions that have caused you to feel rejected in the past. We humans are social animals, and rejection or abandonment is the worst thing that can happen to us. We do everything possible to keep it from happening. When we face the potential of emotional abandonment, our unconscious tactics for avoiding it burst out of their hiding places.

This is the position in which you must once again find yourself if you are going to change brain patterns that keep you from emotional success. In bioenergetic psychoanalysis, you commit to therapy for a predetermined period of time so that when the going gets tough and your fear of abandonment kicks in, you won't run away.

If you decide to go on the life-changing journey of analysis, I will be like a Sherpa with you on the way to the summit of Mt. Everest. It will be your trip, but I know the route, and I know the dangers. I know how to deal with the obstacles and difficulties we will inevitably encounter on the way. I will make sure that you are safe and supported and that your needs are primary. I've made the journey, as a guided traveler and as a guide to other travelers. I know what to expect and how to handle whatever comes our way.

Unlike the Everest of today with its massive crowds, we will be

> You won't come out of bioenergetic psychoanalysis with a checklist to change your behavior, but you will feel different in your own skin, and you will be changed. You will be able to enjoy the beautiful moments of your life while you are in them. You will feel joyful when you are with the people you love, doing things you love to do. A weight will have been lifted from your shoulders and off your chest. The tensions in your body will have been drained out of you. If they return, due to some circumstance life throws at you, you will have skills you can deliberately use to bring yourself back to peace of mind, having been through the process with your therapist many times before. Simply put, you will be happy.

pioneers. Most people still do not make the journey to their highest human potential. Modern conveniences and the promise of quick solutions obscure the masses from seeing that lifelong emotional success requires commitment to a journey. This is the secret, and you are in on it.

At the end of your guided journey, you will have come face-to-face with your worst fears.

You will have uncovered many of your unconscious beliefs. You will have experienced, understood, and embraced your feelings, your prohibitions against them, and the ways they motivated your behavior and your choices. You will have mourned the losses associated with the "wrong" choices you made as a result. You will be able to move forward, making the "right" choices easily. You won't be motivated by mysterious impulses you don't understand or cannot easily figure out.

You won't find yourself, as I once did, sitting outside in the sunshine on a beautiful day, in a gorgeous setting, with people I loved, and thinking, *If I weren't so miserable, I would be incredibly happy right now.*

In short, you will be the happiest, most joyful, most productive, strongest version of yourself that you've ever known.

CHAPTER 4

Bioenergetic Analysis: A Faster Track

In psychoanalysis, as discussed in the previous chapter, the patterns and stresses you experience in your relationships—including the one with your therapist—will be the focus and subject of intense scrutiny and analysis to help you reach your goal of happiness. You might also work on coping strategies, but they will not be the focus of your therapy.

Some therapies focus on the development of coping strategies and techniques. They fall under the general heading of cognitive behavioral therapies and will be helpful if you want basic coaching on how to manage your behaviors.

There is also a class of therapy called existential/humanistic therapy. This type of therapy is meant to help you expand self-awareness and explore spirituality through discussion and mindfulness practices. Unlike psychoanalysis, existential/humanistic therapies concentrate more on intellectual exploration and willful techniques than analyzing your relationship experiences or accessing emotions through bodywork.

In this chapter, the focus is bioenergetic analysis.

In bioenergetic analysis, a therapist will analyze your body to understand your unconscious beliefs and conflicts, and you will engage in stressful physical poses to unleash the emotions that fuel them.

There is no way to hide from feelings in bodywork. That is why change and relief happen more quickly than through psychoanalysis alone.

The Body in Therapy

Bioenergetics treats the body and mind as functionally identical; what goes on in the mind is reflected by what is happening in the body, and vice versa.

Think about it: in your everyday interactions, you can often see a person's body express very different information from what that person is saying. For instance, what do you know about someone who is telling you that she is not angry but who is raising her voice, or someone who says he is fine but whose arms are crossed tightly over his chest?

In psychoanalytic therapy, feelings only arise due to stressful relationship events. This can make the process very slow, especially if clients have strong muscular contractions that prevent emotion from moving through their bodies. Psychoanalysis, by itself, has no system in place to deliberately incite emotion.

For some people, the slower pace of psychoanalysis is right, but for others it's too slow.

There are even people for whom the incorporation of bodywork is essential. It may actually be their only route to achieving self-regulation (the ability to calm down when they're upset and cheer up when they're down). This is regardless of the time they have to devote to therapy.

THE HISTORY OF BIOENERGETIC ANALYSIS

Bioenergetic analysis came out of character analysis, which was developed by Dr. Wilhelm Reich in 1933. Reich, a colleague of Dr. Sigmund Freud, noted that certain character traits or personality traits—people's ways of interacting with the world—are reflected in the body. In his work, Reich focused on breathing to open up a freer way of living.

One of Reich's students, Dr. Alexander Lowen, had undergone his teacher's character analysis in the 1940s. He found it extremely helpful in his life, so much so that he changed careers, leaving law and going to Europe to study medicine and become a medical doctor.

In the 1950s, Dr. Lowen, along with another physician, Dr. John Pierrakos, broadened Reich's idea of analyzing muscular contractions in the breathing apparatus. Their work became bioenergetic analysis, the analysis of contractions all over the body. They worked with bands of tension starting at the top of the head and going down the body to the pelvis. Lowen believed that muscular contractions represented energy we use to hold back action in the body.

In general, very subtle and deeply held emotions are never accessed without bodywork, regardless of how many talk sessions you have or how long you talk.

CHRONIC TENSION: A WAY OF LIFE

Every stress produces a state of tension in your body. Normally, that tension disappears when the stress is relieved. Chronic tensions, however, persist after the provoking stress has been removed, and they make the body look and feel the way it does. As I explained in chapter 2, this process begins in infancy.

Over time, as you continuously hold back certain feelings, chronic muscular tensions disturb your emotional health by decreasing your energy, restricting your movement, and limiting your self-expression.

There are so many examples of chronic tension in the body that an entire book could be devoted to the possibilities.

Here are some basic examples of how strategies to hold back emotions in childhood become your habitual behavior, the unconscious ways you hold your body, and the way you are.

Some people habitually contract their throats. Maybe they were told they talked too loudly when they were young or were often ridiculed for what they said. As a result, they learned to tighten their throats to hold back the sound. In extreme cases, their constricted throat might give them a much higher voice than they would otherwise have had. Some of my male clients have found that after they have released an enormous amount of anger in therapy,

An example is the wish to strike out. Think of a two-year-old who is angry. What does the child want to do? She wants to reach out and hit. To keep herself from hitting, she has to contract her back, shoulder, and chest muscles. If this happens often enough and the child has no other means to express her aggressive energy, these contractions will become her way of being. This will be reflected in the way her body looks or feels in the back, shoulders, and chest areas.

Lowen's bioenergetic analysis enjoyed a heyday in the 1970s. It was very exciting to practitioners because it is such a powerful way to quickly release feeling and provide a large sense of relief and calm afterward. But some were not properly trained to help people handle their flood of feelings following bodywork.

When you engage the body, it's easy to open people up, but helping them to move forward in a healthy way takes a good deal of training. In the early days, bioenergetic analysis was offered too casually, without the proper guidance to help clients understand what was happening once their feelings had been released. This is why bioenergetic analysis fell out of favor. People training to be bioenergetic analysts today must undergo bioenergetic analysis themselves and, ideally, extensive training in psychoanalysis.

Currently, body-centered psychotherapies are becoming popular again as research bears out the reality that many issues cannot be resolved with talk therapy alone, if at all.

Trauma is among the most extreme of those issues. However, any life experience that involves fear, helplessness, or the feeling of being overwhelmed, no matter how subtle, at any age, can create symptoms that cannot be helped by talk therapy and coping strategies alone.

Thankfully, research has brought scientific validity to bioenergetic analysis. It is a practice that has been providing effective relief and helping people to have happier, more vibrant and productive lives for over sixty years.

their throats have opened up, and they have much deeper, more resonant voices.

Neck tension that creates headaches is also a result of holding back crying, yelling, sadness, or rage. If you learned, as a child, not to reach out for affection, if you were not picked up when you asked, or if you were slapped down emotionally when you reached for comfort, you learned to hold back that impulse. You might have held your arms at your side against the impulse to reach, creating a lot of tension in your shoulders and neck.

As an adult, you will still have contraction in those muscles. You will hold your shoulders stiffly all day, not even realizing you are doing so. If you experience a trigger in the present that activates an old desire to reach out, you will probably experience an intensity of symptoms in that area, including headaches.

You might have stiffness in your back, hips, or ankles; bad knees or arthritis; or poor digestion. These can be purely physical in origin, but often, they have an emotional component. Your ability to have easy, enjoyable interactions with a variety of people might be impaired because so many things that other people do and say trigger feelings of discomfort, frustration, or anger in you.

When you explode over traffic, the intensity of your feeling is rarely about the traffic. It's often unconscious anger you feel about something in the past, over which you had no control. You were held back from getting what you wanted or getting where you needed to go. The circumstances of past deprivation are different for every person. You might have needed respect, predictability, control, or consistency. Your unique story will contain the details.

The bottom line is that your anger might be about traffic, on the surface, but the intensity of your anger is about something else. At its heart, your explosion is the expression of intense feelings about something else—from the past—that you generally manage in a rational way but, for whatever reason, the traffic brought out.

AN ENERGY DRAIN

You are human, not the Hoover Dam. Your body was not meant to hold a massive buildup of energy over a long period of time. Everything that enters, or is generated by, your body is meant to flow out of it again. If you think you can indefinitely hold back all that energy with your will, you are trying to defy this fundamental physical reality. You will fail.

You will be a person with road rage or something else equally irrational. Or you might be easily susceptible to illness or accident prone.

I know it might sound crazy when I say that your attempts to hold back that energy affect your life and your happiness, but think about it. Holding back an expression of feeling with your muscles *all the time* takes energy.

Let's say your shoulders can theoretically bear the weight of one hundred pounds. Now let's say you always unconsciously tense your shoulders to hold back a desire that is unacceptable to express. That tension costs you energy and strength. If the isometric of holding takes the equivalent of fifty pounds of energy, then you have only fifty pounds of energy left. That's only half what should be available for reaching out and getting what you want in life (or pushing back against something that you don't want).

Muscle contraction takes energy. Unnecessary muscle contraction sustained for long periods of time makes you weaker than you would be otherwise, emotionally and physically.

It is common in our culture to separate the emotional and the physical, but this is not how our bodies work. If you feel tired because you did not get a lot of sleep the night before, you are physically tired and emotionally tired. Emotional energy and physical energy—it's really all energy. They are not separate.

Energy used to hold back unconscious emotion through chronic muscular contraction is stolen energy that you could be using to get through the day.

Using Your Body in Psychotherapy

To achieve lasting results, then, you must change your body. You need to relieve chronic tension and learn the method that puts you in charge of keeping future tension from building up.

Bioenergetics will put you in charge of removing the "load on your back" and the "weight on your shoulders." It will give you the skills to avoid getting "hung up" on things and the means to get "out of your head."

No therapy gets rid of feelings, but what you learn in bioenergetic analysis will teach you how to disarm their power to overwhelm you or to fuel certain beliefs that undermine you.

You will be aware of, be able to manage, and be able to use your feelings to help you make wise decisions.

> During bioenergetic analysis you will, literally, integrate different parts of your brain by tuning in to mental, physical, and emotional aspects of yourself that were previously out of your awareness. You will elicit memories and emotions through stressful physical positions, and you will learn to manage your feelings by embodying them consciously rather than separating them from your conscious awareness. When those memories and feelings become part of your conscious life story, you will end up with more choices about the way you live your life. You will no longer be motivated by unknown parts of yourself.

You will rarely, if ever, be subject to emotional manipulation by others or unknown beliefs inside you. You will not get overwhelmed by your emotions so that you lose conscious control of your behavior. Instead, you will have true mastery over your actions; they will not master you. You will be able to allow any feeling to exist in your consciousness without worrying that it will be apparent to others and make you look the fool. You will understand how to use your feelings strategically for your own benefit to get what you want in life.

I'm sure that using your body to access feelings in psychotherapy may still sound pretty weird. Therapy has always been billed as the talking cure. What does that have to do with your body? You talk, and a therapist takes notes and gives you advice, right?

Nope. Surprise! *Feeling* your emotions is key to your success, and here's why.

If you *only* talk in therapy, you will never have the opportunity to experience and change your habit of avoiding your feelings. You will never be able to analyze how your feelings are fueling negative beliefs. And you will never be able to wash them out of you so they don't power negative beliefs in the future.

You will continue to feel stuck, bored, depressed, anxious, or disconnected and never know why. Or you will find that your feelings come blasting out of you when you feel provoked. You'll look as if you have an anger problem or you're "too emotional."

Controlling your feelings so well that you cannot let them move through at an appropriate time and place will keep you exactly the same as you are right now.

You will never be different. And you will never achieve lasting happiness, peace of mind, or emotional satisfaction.

REGAINING YOUR ENERGY THROUGH BIOENERGETIC EXERCISES

Jessica came to me after a terrible breakup.

She was in graduate school, embarking on summer classes. She had found she could not go anywhere or do much of anything. She was actually doubled over with stomach pain and explained that this was a typical way for her to experience stress.

Much of her energy was tied up in her belly, and she was, basically, unable to move.

As she sat with me, I could feel her tension. She was angry and completely overwhelmed. I asked her how she felt about screaming, as this is one of the tools we use in bioenergetic analysis. She agreed to try. (Some people will not, as they have an internal prohibition against vocalizing in this way.)

I had Jessica stand so she could feel the strength of her legs and "ground," which means she could, literally, dissipate excess energy—as a lightning rod does—through her feet as she screamed. I directed her to scream as much as she wanted.

She screamed six times at the top of her lungs and then sat and reflected. We talked about ways she could use screaming and other bioenergetics techniques to handle excess energy that developed as her experience of the breakup unfolded.

When she came back to my office two days later, Jessica said, "It really made a difference! My stomach feels so much better." Then she repeated the exercise, as well as others.

At her next session, she explained that, over the weekend, she had become even more relaxed. She was able to focus, and she had gone back to attending her classes and doing her assignments. She felt she was finally moving forward.

Although this example describes someone who needed help because she was completely unable to take action, don't misunderstand. Bioenergetic analysis is also very helpful to people for whom action is not a problem.

You may be unable to harness your energy for use at the right times and places to get what you need, to protect yourself, or to enjoy life to its fullest.

You *can know* why you explode in anger at inappropriate times or to the wrong people. You *can take back* the energy wasted on that sort of thing and use it to have more of what feels good. You *can crack* the code of any of your seemingly irrational behaviors and undesirable emotional states.

When you do, you won't have to feel embarrassed, ashamed, or like a robot just going through the motions of life.

Bioenergetic analysis will help you uncover resources stronger than any you have known before and will move you toward being the happiest, most powerful version of yourself possible. On the way, you will acquire self-knowledge and self-acceptance that leads to greater peace of mind.

You may be thinking, *I do know myself, and I'm fine with who I am*. But if you don't feel joy and you don't have peace of mind or emotional satisfaction, you don't fully know yourself. Beliefs and feelings inside you that elude your consciousness are keeping you from experiencing the life you want.

Historically, bioenergetic analysts have focused on analyzing and relieving chronic muscular contractions through bodywork rather than "talking" to help you. By focusing on the body, bioenergetic analysis brings faster relief from specific problems than nearly any other form of psychotherapy,

However, it's not perfect, and it shares one major downside with most forms of psychotherapy: it does not necessarily bring lasting happiness and peace of mind. That's why, in my practice, I combine bioenergetic analysis with psychoanalysis to get lasting results. Psychoanalysis creates lasting change, and bioenergetic analysis creates faster change.

Bioenergetic psychoanalysis *will* help you achieve lasting happiness, emotional satisfaction, and peace of mind when you commit to it.

If the whole process still sounds a little theoretical or far-fetched to you, I assure you it is not. The next chapters will help you better understand exactly what happens when you are doing it and demonstrate how it can help you.

CHAPTER 5

What to Expect from Bioenergetic Bodywork

Make a fist as tight as you can and hold it for one minute. When you relax the tension, notice how your fingers will not open back up. They want to stay curled and stiff against any pressure to move them back to their open position.

Now, imagine having done that for practically *(insert your age here)* years and then trying to put your fingers back in their proper place. It wouldn't be easy, would it? And it would be uncomfortable. In fact, you might not believe your fingers were supposed to move that way. But if you did the work to get them moving, imagine how much more you could do with that hand.

It's the same all over your body!

EXPECT SOME PAIN!

Bioenergetic bodywork is uncomfortable. Quite honestly, that is the idea. To change, you have to get out of your comfort zone. You are going to find yourself in poses that feel awkward, and you are going to stretch parts of your body you believe should not be stretched that way. You are going to say, "My body doesn't move like that."

And up to now, you were right. But you want change, and change requires—well—change.

Your initial impulse will be to run from or fight the discomfort of the bioenergetic stress poses.

Once you get past that impulse and give in to them, you'll find that seemingly random thoughts and feelings will begin to occur to you. Yes, you *will* feel pain as you stretch, but there's *more* than pain in those chronic muscular contractions.

After the initial difficulty of a pose, you will become conscious of things such as irritation, anger, fear, sadness, or confusion. These are clues about what was going on when the muscular contraction initially formed in your body, long ago.

Images, random thoughts or ideas, and memories will come to mind. You might suddenly experience a feeling that you cannot explain. You might burst out laughing hysterically, cry, or feel enraged and not know why. You might suddenly flash on a baby lying in a crib by itself, screaming its head off. You will probably have no idea what this image is about or believe it has anything to do with you. But this is the beginning.

This is the point at which you are starting to reconnect conscious memories and the energy trapped in chronic muscular contractions in your body. Lifelong happiness is coming within your grasp.

A client in a stress pose once asked me, "Why does it have to be painful? It doesn't make sense to put myself through this!" His anger was real, but it was also a significant memory.

Remember I told you that intensity of anger toward traffic is not really about the traffic but about something else instead? This client's anger was demonstrating the same thing. It was a right-brain, or *implicit*, memory (you will learn more about this in chapter 6) that was being *transferred* to his experience in the stress pose.

At the same time, an *explicit*, or left-brain, memory occurred to him. He remembered having suffered as a child to achieve goals set by his mother. The right and left sides of his brain were revealing memories in tandem.

This was his opportunity to integrate right- and left-brain memories by expressing fully and directly—without fear of repercussion—the anger in the current situation and the memory of his suffering in his past. He had held it in for many years, numbing himself to do so.

But he couldn't let it out. It did not make sense to him to express his anger in the present about something in the past. His mother's goals for him had, after all, been reasonable. His well-developed defense against emotional expression kept him from releasing the anger in my office. He could not relax his prohibition against expression of an "irrational" feeling.

There is a time and place for every emotion.

A therapist's office is the place for "irrational" expression of feelings you were never allowed to directly express in the past. Accepting this reality is part of the pain of therapy. The longer it takes for you to accept, the longer the journey takes. Don't waste your time.

CASE EXAMPLES

CHANGING BRAIN PATHWAYS

James was the owner of a fast-growing tech company. He was in his midthirties, very competent, and financially successful. An amiable, agreeable person, he got along well with people; he was good-looking and very athletic. In short, you might think he had it all. He came to me, though, because he was having trouble getting out of a current, unsatisfying relationship and was disturbed about what a long-term relationship would be like, given his mind-set in this current relationship.

Overall, James was confident about his work life and his abilities. He was positive about life, in general, but he also felt that there was something wrong. His relationship was unsatisfying, and he was doing more and more to get away from it through work and other social activities. It seemed like any other goal he had to deal with. He felt an obligation to this relationship even though it was not satisfying. He wanted out, but he felt he should make it work because it looked the way relationships are supposed to look.

He said, "I work, work, work. I never make time to enjoy myself or feel pleasure at all. In fact, I sometimes worry that I'm not going to be able to make time for my family when I have one. I don't make time for fun." Basically, he didn't feel any real happiness in his life.

As we talked, I saw that James had some gut instincts that he verbalized but was not able to act on. He knew he wanted to leave the relationship but was stuck in his head on all the rights and wrongs. He was pushing through every day, feeling generally unsatisfied, unhappy, and numb. He felt stuck, emotionally.

In traditional talk therapy, James might have been encouraged to talk through all the logical reasons why he might want to stay in the relationship or end it. But he was already a master at thinking logically and making the "right decisions." He did not need a therapist for that. James was unfulfilled and stuck in his head, not feeling emotion. To help him move forward and enjoy life, we needed to get him out of his head.

Bodywork was the answer. It starts by simply focusing on your body and any sensations that are present, such as tensions and places that feel weak.

You might stand instead of sitting for a portion of the therapy, seeing if it makes you uncomfortable and exploring how and why. You might even stand in a stressful pose and allow your muscles to vibrate, or you might pound on a foam cube. Nothing I suggest you do is required. I explain an exercise first and ask you to explore how you feel about it, so you can refuse if you want.

I asked James, "What do you think about the idea of involving your body?" He said, "My feelings aren't in my body. My feelings are in my mind." His idea begged an incredibly important point.

You notice your feelings with your mind, but when you do that, you are actually recognizing what's happening in your body.

We are not just using metaphors when we say things such as "You make me sick," "I have a gut feeling about her," "My heart longs for you," or "That sends shivers up my spine." These are real physical reactions. Emotion comes from a Latin word that means, "to move out," or "stir up." It is, literally, the movement of energy. You cannot have a feeling if something doesn't move in your body.

Something called a vagus nerve relays to your brain massive amounts of information about what's happening in your body. When that happens, you register a feeling or an emotion. This process might make you think that you've had that feeling in your brain, but it has actually occurred in your body. Once James understood the connection, he wanted to try bodywork.

To begin, I asked him to stand in the *basic bioenergetic pose* (Figure 5.1) and to notice and report anything he could about his body. In this pose, you stand with your feet shoulder-width apart, toes straight forward, knees slightly bent, shoulders, chest, and belly relaxed. At the same time, you breathe deeply with your mouth slightly open.

I wanted James to become familiar with the process of paying attention to body sensations and letting them guide him. This is part of the foundation of bioenergetic analysis.

Figure 5.1: Basic bioenergetic pose

I said, "Notice how your legs feel as you stand. Feel their strength. Feel what it's like to shift your weight from one leg to the other, and notice the tension as it moves from one leg to the other. Notice how deeply you're breathing into your belly. Notice if you are holding your shoulders up or down. Notice whether there is tension in your jaw or not. Scan for tension in other parts of your body."

I then directed James into the traditional assessment pose of bio-energetic analysis, called the *bow pose* (as in archery) (Figure 5.2). To do so, I asked him to make fists, place them in the small of his back, and make a bow of his body by bending backward.

Stiffness in his upper body and hips diminished James's ability to arch backward with ease. His chest and belly were extremely rigid, revealing deep muscular tension. While he looked fit and attractive,

Figure 5.2: Bow pose

rigidity of this kind without complementary flexibility is the physical manifestation of the life problems he was describing. His ability to breathe deeply was greatly diminished, and correspondingly, so was his capacity to feel anything, including happiness.

This gave me a big clue about what to focus on in his bodywork.

I asked James if he would mind using the breathing stool, an important tool in bioenergetic analysis. It is a bar-height stool with a rounded foam top. You lean backward over it from a standing position to stretch your contracted muscles and loosen up. When that happens, you will breathe more deeply and bring more oxygen into your body. You will naturally begin to *feel* more, especially feelings of your heart. James agreed to lean over the breathing stool. Because of his deep tension, he felt a good deal of pain at first. I told him, "Try not to run from the pain, and try not to fight it. Allow yourself to feel it, open your mouth and throat, and vocalize any pain you feel. Say 'ahh,' make coughing sounds, or do whatever your impulse is. In doing so, your chest will loosen up. You will begin to breathe more, and you will begin to feel more. Pay attention to any images, thoughts, and sensations that come up, even if they seem random."

Picture James leaning backward over the breathing stool at about heart level (Figure 5.3). His feet are flat on the floor, his arms are over his head, and his knees are shoulder-width apart. He is breathing and

Figure 5.3: Breathing stool

allowing himself to feel the stretch and pain of the posture.

After thirty seconds, he comes off the stool by sliding toward the floor. Then he stands slowly and hangs his torso forward, with knees slightly bent and feet shoulder-width apart. Gravity pulls his head and his arms in the opposite direction, giving his body a bit of a break, and he breathes deeply into

Figure 5.4: Grounding pose

his belly. This is called the *grounding pose* (Figure 5.4).

Next, I asked James to stand facing the wall and put his hands on the wall above his head, bend his knees, and lean forward so as to stretch all of the muscles around his neck and shoulders. I call this pose the *hammock* (Figure 5.5). I then asked him to drop his head and take about five breaths. As he did this, I instructed, "Notice what this feels like. Notice if it's hard for you, or if it creates some pain for you. Notice any sensations in your body."

Figure 5.5: Hammock

Figure 5.6: Skier's pose

Then, I helped him assume a *skier's pose* (Figure 5.6), leaning his back against the wall and bending his knees as if he were sitting in a chair or skiing down a mountain. I asked him to stay as long as possible in that position and to notice how he managed the sensations. He said, "It's pain. It doesn't matter if it hurts. You deal with it."

Having introduced James to several of the bodywork poses to familiarize him with using his body in therapy, I asked if he was willing to do some more work over the breathing stool. He agreed.

When he was over the stool, I directed James to breathe as deeply as possible, with his mouth open. I told him that when the pain got to be more than he wanted to tolerate, he should slide down toward the floor and rest a moment and then slowly stand again, take five or six deep breaths, and repeat the process. As he got accustomed to the experience, I told him, "Allow yourself to stay on the stool longer than you think you can. Vocalizing will help you do this."

James did not want to vocalize. In fact, many people do not. They are used to silently dealing with their pain, and they believe that vocalizing reveals weakness. Leaning backward and making sounds, especially in front of a stranger, can cause people to feel embarrassed and vulnerable. They have never heard of doing this before, and they certainly have never done it before. Frankly, it feels kind of ridiculous and irrational.

We have all been taught not to reveal the pain we feel, especially in front of others. We have been taught to manage our emotions silently. This strategy is great . . . up to a point.

Being taught that there is never a time and a place for all feelings, we don't allow ourselves to "let down" and let out our pain. James was no different. He was a man who could stand a lot of pain, and he had gotten that way by numbing himself.

I explained all this to James and encouraged him to use the opportunity to acknowledge and release any pain he felt.

Each time he went over the stool, he got a little deeper into the stretch. He bent over the stool for thirty seconds, then for a minute, then a minute and a half, then two minutes, then three minutes. The last and longest time he went over the stool, he allowed himself to release a sound that was a kind of coughing laugh that eventually turned into a sob. James allowed himself to continue crying the rest of the time he was bent over the stool. Later, he reported that while he cried, the physical pain of bending over the stool had left him.

Once he was off the stool and up from the grounding pose, James was clear-headed. He wanted to sit on the couch and talk about what came to his mind.

James had entered a state of complete relaxation, which he said he did not remember feeling before. He said that he was having memories and accessing emotions that were connecting him to past experiences and beliefs that were driving him as an adult. He said it was his first awareness of these thoughts and feelings as drivers for him.

He had let out some of the stuff inside that had been keeping him from feeling positive about his life. This stuff had led him to make all his decisions based on what he believed was logical reasoning rather than wisdom from his intuition and feelings. In other words, after going over the stool, he had become more flexible in thinking about his life. He had broken out of the rigid logic that had been motivating him for as long as he could remember.

As bodywork continued over several sessions, James would get mad about the physical pain he was feeling. He'd say, "I don't understand why this has to hurt. What's the point?"

In one session, he recalled saying similar things to his mother when he was a child. She had pushed him hard, which had been very difficult and painful for him. It had also made him very angry, but he had held in much of his frustration and anger toward her. He had believed she was right and that he was supposed to "just do it," so he had submitted.

It is not unusual for us, as young children, to be convinced and coerced to work extra hard in order to achieve a better future. We cannot be angry and frustrated, because we're only being asked to do what is right for us. We know this and believe it, but we also still feel a lot of anger that has no place to go.

We have to hold that anger in, and that is exactly what James did. It made him the very hardworking, successful person he was. Of course, he may have been that kind of person anyway; we'll never know. All we know is that he did hold in that anger. He'd been containing those feelings for much of his life, and it had affected his happiness.

As more memories and feelings came to his consciousness during our sessions, James realized that he was doing things he was *supposed* to do with his personal life rather than doing what he might *like* to do. We all have to do things we don't want to do to reach goals, but for James, that was *all* he could do. He was holding his body so tightly that he could never let down. He could not feel the joy or access the wisdom of his body that comes with relaxation. He was rigidly following rules that did not work for him.

Through our work, James started getting insight and loosening his rigid muscles and the corresponding inflexible logic. He realized that he tightened up to tolerate things that were painful and frustrating. And he realized that this response was part of why he felt stuck.

James did ten sessions of bodywork over five months, weekly at first, and then less often. We did not use the breathing stool each time, but it was key for uncovering insight and releasing much of the tension that was previously making him inflexible to change.

We did *talk* about his feelings and how to put them into perspective, but the tools of bodywork let James know the truth of his body—what he was really feeling—at a deeper level than merely talking could have ever done. Once he felt this truth and understood it, he was free to use it to his advantage.

Within those five months of therapy, James ended his relationship and found ways to balance his work and pleasure activities more to his liking. He also began a new relationship that was more fulfilling to him than any prior relationship ever had been. He found himself living and communicating with a level of feeling that he had not thought possible. He was following his instincts regarding decision making.

He believed that he had deeper concerns to work on, but he was satisfied with the way things were at that time and believed that he

had some tools he could use to shake himself loose if he were to feel stuck again.

To change, we have to make new brain pathways. James is a good example of this process in action. His trouble with expressing feelings developed early in his relationship with his parents. (Parents are the experts and authorities on how to be a civilized human being.) At that time, certain beliefs—brain pathways—were established about how to be and how to be acceptable. To change those deeply held, unconscious beliefs, James needed to break the patterns.

Doing so through bodywork accelerated this change. James began to be comfortable feeling his emotions as they moved through him rather than feeling overwhelmed by them or compelled to do something about them. This created a happier, more flexible man. Being satisfied with the relief he felt at the time, James left therapy.

Without longer exposure to new patterns of thinking and feeling, new brain pathways can give way to the old ones in times of stress. However, the relief that clients feel from short-term work after having been miserable for a long time is often enough. That was the case for James. Even though he believed he had more to address, he was not ready to commit.

I suspected that if James were to become unsatisfied with his new relationship or with the relationship unfolding with his future children, he would come back. As it turned out, he did come back, about six months later, deciding that he wanted more lasting satisfaction and happiness.

Committing to long-term work may not feel worth doing unless you believe you might lose everything that is important to you or feel that your current life is unbearable. But you don't need to let things get that bad. After all, you wouldn't let things go that far down the tubes in business, so why would you do it to yourself? Hire a professional.

Getting Grounded in a Time of Stress

Another client who gained great relief from bodywork was Julia, a college senior in her last semester before graduation. Unlike James, Julia had felt perfectly happy and content with her life as it was. She considered herself a decent student and felt good overall, personally and socially. She saw herself as intelligent, confident, physically fit, and able to do the things that she wanted to do.

Julia had always been very social, but she started having a lot of difficulty sleeping, and she also began to feel self-conscious in social interactions. She felt awkward all the time. She even began to have anxiety attacks when she was around people, including her friends. Julia had lost her confidence. She was very unsure of herself, her social life was going downhill, and she felt completely overwhelmed.

As Julia answered some initial questions about her history and family, she revealed that she was a person who had never wanted to have anything to do with feelings. When she was a kid, she'd get angry when her mother asked her to "feel stuff." She'd say, "I don't want to talk about that, Mom." She was very clear about this aspect of herself. She considered herself to be very strong but came to see me because she felt she had lost her footing and was not above asking for help to regain it.

As a way of introducing bodywork to Julia, I explained that the majority of communication is nonverbal. It is sent by eye contact, facial expression, posture, gesture, and the speed and tone of voice used when talking. Though none of these communications are word-based messages, they all provide information we use to understand one another and to communicate things we are not conscious of in ourselves.

Julia wanted to understand what she was communicating non-verbally and find other, less disruptive, ways to do so. Being athletic, she agreed to try bodywork right away.

Initially, I asked Julia to breathe while standing in the basic bio-energetic pose and notice what she could about her body to take an inventory of what was happening inside. I asked, "How does it feel to be standing here? You don't have to answer my questions. But pay attention as I direct your focus. What do you notice about your body as you breathe? Do you feel any areas of tension?" She mentioned some tension in her shoulders.

At that point, I asked her to move into the bow pose. If you recall, this posture allows me to see how a person responds to the stress of the pose and thus to get a broad snapshot of tension in the body. I could see that Julia struggled with arching her upper body backward, due to tension.

Next, I asked her to face the wall, place her hands high on the wall, shoulder-width apart, and let her head hang heavily between her extended arms in the hammock pose. I asked her to make any vocalizations that she wanted or to breathe louder or deeper as she went into the stretch. I told her that if she could allow herself to feel pain that was there and express it through vocalizing, it would dissipate. When she finished, Julia reported feeling a deep relaxation fill her upper body. She liked the hammock pose.

I next asked Julia to get into the skier's pose against the wall and allow her legs to tire and vibrate. I asked her to hold that position until she wanted to sit down or stand up. At that point she was to raise her back and reduce some of the tension on her legs. I asked her to continue moving her back up the wall as the tension grew until she was standing almost upright and her legs were vibrating gently. This vibration would allow her to consciously experience and focus on the energy in her legs.

Next, I asked Julia to bend over the breathing stool so it supported her back at midchest level. I hoped to open up the muscles of her torso. This would allow more oxygen into her body and stretch

> Muscle vibrations induced by some of the poses can cause you to feel as if you're losing control. The shaking can be physically difficult to tolerate and can induce anxiety. You might want to tighten your muscles and stop the vibration. Ideally, you will allow the vibrations to continue. You will find that you are not losing control but, instead, are experiencing a stream of feelings that connect you consciously to the full strength of your energy and power. Nothing in the poses is cause for anxiety.

her chest muscles. (These muscles are used to protect us from fear of attack by others for not being good enough, ideas that were in Julia's head and disrupting her life.) Julia felt a lack of confidence. When you don't feel confident, you protect yourself by arching your body forward like an animal with its back up, protecting its soft underbelly.

While Julia was over the stool, I asked her not to fight the pain. Instead, I told her to feel it and express any feelings she had by opening her mouth and throat and verbalizing to whatever degree she felt comfortable.

She bent back over the breathing stool twice, for about a minute each time. She breathed loudly. Some people might shout, moan, or cry. Julia did not.

After the breathing stool, I asked her to take the basic grounding pose and to breathe deeply into her belly while relaxing her upper body.

Julia found the grounding pose to be very helpful. She was too "up in her head," and she knew it. She overanalyzed herself and everything she said and did. She was having a crisis of confidence because of a running tape in her head that said, *Oh, did I say that right?* and *What are people thinking?* She had lost connection to her strength and, with it, her ability to let her head go and be herself.

Julia was a physically strong person so she was easily able to hold the grounding pose for three minutes. She then rolled up very slowly, one vertebra at a time, keeping her head heavy until she was standing upright. To finish, she brought her head up and then breathed into her belly for another minute, standing and reflecting.

When we had completed the bodywork at this session, Julia sat on the couch and we talked. She made connections between the feelings in her body and how those feelings related to other aspects of her life that she was thinking about after the bodywork.

Many thoughts came into her mind spontaneously since the energy in her body was moving more freely. The poses had loosened muscle contractions. Clients often remark how interesting it is that so many thoughts automatically come to mind after doing bodywork exercises. They say things such as, "Wow, what a funny thing to come up. I haven't thought of that in years!"

Julia started talking about early experiences with her family, difficulties she was having with her peers, how hard it was to think about her future after graduation, everything that she had to get done, and her difficulties with anxiety and sleeping at night. This first session allowed her to open up her feelings about the difficult life situation she was facing as graduation approached.

I sent Julia home with instructions to do the breathing stool technique over an exercise stability ball twice a day, as it would help her reduce the anxiety attacks she was having.

During an anxiety attack, you don't breathe, or you breathe so fast that you do not get enough oxygen into your body. By bending backward over the edge of a couch, over a foam roller, over a piece of four-inch PVC pipe, over a barstool with a pillow on it, or over anything else to open up your chest, you will start breathing. You must also consciously reconnect with the reality of your body by grounding. You can do so by rolling your feet on golf balls, which I suggested that Julia do. Lastly, I suggested that she incorporate the grounding pose into her schedule every day for at least five minutes twice a day.

Julia returned for her second session and said, "I'm sleeping better. And I was in a situation where I got really anxious, but I used some of the techniques that you shared with me, and I was able to make it through without having to leave."

She had found the grounding pose to be incredibly powerful and useful. She felt how it allowed her to connect to the strength of her lower body, where her steadiness, her power, and her stability lay. She had recognized this after doing the grounding pose the very first time.

By her third session, Julia was feeling much better. She was back to feeling confident and not feeling weird with her friends. She was sleeping better at night, not having anxiety attacks, and no longer feeling socially awkward. She said, "This has really helped." She decided that the impending graduation had thrown her off balance and that the bodywork had definitely helped her find her strength again.

In the face of her upcoming life change, Julia had, initially, used her go-to tactic of avoiding feelings about it. But this didn't work. Her feelings were too strong. Her fear broke through and started showing up in a place that did not make sense: her social life.

As Julia reconnected to her strength and became grounded in her body through bodywork, she could consciously acknowledge the fear she had about moving into adulthood. As a result, the other anxieties fell away. She settled back into feeling more normal and regained her ability to move forward in her day-to-day life.

Julia's experience points out a huge advantage of bodywork. She and I could have talked through many sessions. I could have taught her cognitive tricks to combat the lack of confidence, and they might have helped. Instead, the trick was to engage her body in a direct way, to connect her to the strength of her legs while "letting go" of her head. It was exactly what she needed to discover the underlying trouble. It only took three hours in the office.

As James did, Julia knew that there was more work she could do, but she was not interested. She had gotten the relief she wanted and was satisfied. She also was surprised and happy that she had achieved her goal and felt so much better so quickly and effectively.

The speed of Julia's progress was supported by two important factors. When she began, she was already capable of tolerating a large amount of energy moving through her body. That kept her from being easily overwhelmed by feelings that came up. Even if she didn't like them, she could physically handle them.

She was also able to consciously acknowledge with relative ease her fears about life after graduation and admit that they were at the root of her anxiety. Had these two things not been working in Julia's favor, the process could have taken much longer.

A SLOWER INTRODUCTION TO BODYWORK

Since bodywork is so powerful, I do not use it with every client. I'm cautious to discern who might benefit from bodywork right away and who might benefit more from other therapy techniques, or at least a very slow introduction of bodywork. If I suspect that someone might be overwhelmed by the results of bodywork, I begin by getting them to notice what it's like to breathe and feel their body.

Rachel, for example, was highly educated and understood things on an intellectual level incredibly fast. This gave her a sense of control. It was how she succeeded in life. She came to me because she was very, very unhappy. She had undergone "a lot" of therapy, which she told me hadn't worked. She was leaving a relationship she had been in for many years but that had been unsatisfying for about 90 percent of the time. She felt, overall, that "life is miserable. I'm absolutely, completely unhappy."

Mind you, anyone interacting with Rachel would think that she was smashingly happy. She was a beautiful, successful writer, well-off, and smart. But she felt none of these things.

Rachel had a sister close in age and a much older brother. She had had a very "cushy" childhood, materially, but she had felt totally ignored by her mother and terrified by her loud, alcoholic father. She felt her mother loved and paid more attention to her sister than to her. Rachel was a very small person and looked almost like a teenager, although she was in her late thirties. She was energetic and loved physical activities. However, she lacked vitality and looked almost breakable.

 Whereas Julia needed to be grounded to get out of her head, Rachel needed to be grounded to build her strength and power. It was as if she were completely disconnected from her body.

I explained that bodywork would be beneficial, but connecting to her body needed to be done very slowly. She wanted to give it a try.

To help Rachel feel the foundation of her strength and build her vitality, we needed to start at her feet. I had her roll her feet on golf balls, pushing her feet into them and feeling the pain. As she did this, I asked her to open her mouth to vocalize what she felt.

Our feet are our connection with the ground, and the ground is where our strength comes from. It's our connection with the earth. If we release the tension in our feet, we strengthen our foundation. In other words, we are grounding ourselves.

Rachel was not a person who registered feeling consciously, so when she did this grounding exercise, she did not cry out. In fact, she did not vocalize at all. She only breathed.

Generally, I ask someone to stand in the bow pose before doing anything else, as an assessment. With Rachel I felt that grounding was important before I asked her to stand in the vulnerable position of the bow.

When she did stand in the bow pose, Rachel's body revealed tension throughout, and she was nearly overwhelmed by the intensity of feeling evoked. This corresponded with the overall sense I had of her. If she were to open up her feelings at any level, she would be too overwhelmed by them to want to continue in future sessions.

Given this assessment, I decided to maintain a focus on building her strength and getting her grounded. I did this first by having her stand in the skier's pose against the wall for a lengthy period of time. This allowed her to develop and feel vibration in her legs.

Then I asked her to stand in the grounding pose and to maintain it as long as possible. I wanted her to be very conscious of and to focus on her legs holding her up. I also wanted her to notice what it felt like to relax her neck as she breathed deeply into her belly.

I thought Rachel would feel anxious in the grounding pose, and she did. This is because I was asking her to let go of her head, which was the only way she maintained a feeling of control over her life and her interactions with the world.

At the end of that first session, Rachel told me that she felt as if she had not really achieved anything. She decided to return but was skeptical.

I asked her if she would be willing to do exercises at home before the next session, and she was. So I told her to continue working with the golf balls (or tennis balls, if that were more agreeable) every day. I also suggested that she do the skier's and grounding poses twice each day for at least two minutes.

Upon her return the next week, she had not done any of the home exercises. She felt defeated and saw no point in anything.

In this second session we repeated the bodywork. Then we talked about why she did not want to do the exercises at home. We tried to figure out what might make her decide to do them. She doubted the whole experience, the whole mode of therapy. In fact, she did not believe that anything at all would work.

Rachel felt totally unable to face the world, which was exactly why she needed to repeat the process of connecting to the strength in her legs and letting go of the tensions in her foundation, her feet. She needed to "let herself go" in the grounding pose over and over. That would let her build strength in her legs and gain the strength to tolerate the intense emotions that would inevitably come when she began working with the tension all over her body.

After six weeks of one visit per week, Rachel said, "Okay, I think I can trust this. I do feel a little more confident." She slowly began to trust in the process and in me a little more, which was a lot for her. It was a good sign that more changes were to come.

Happiness for the Long Term

Paul was a talented and technically capable artist who was supporting himself well. He was classically handsome, physically fit, and full of appreciation for beauty in the world and his success in life. He made friends easily and had experienced long-term intimate relationships with several people. He had recently found the woman of his dreams, but he came to me saying he was unreasonably unhappy. He thought life was supposed to feel better than what he was experiencing. He also had a tendency to turn away from difficult emotional situations rather than face them. This was affecting not only his personal life at times but some business decisions as well.

Paul was one of five children. He had a very sweet mother, but one who was not very attentive, preferring to do her own thing. His father was an overachieving, high-powered businessman who was a raging, abusive alcoholic. One of Paul's concerns was that he had a tendency to yield without resistance to people who were being unreasonable or overbearing or who he believed were more powerful than he was. He would walk away from some lucrative jobs or refuse to talk to the people he loved. He knew this way of responding was irrational, but he could not make himself act differently.

Paul's therapy began with the usual introduction to bodywork, as described with James, Julia, and Rachel. But Paul was more interested in obtaining lasting happiness and overall peace of mind than a short-term solution for a particular pressing problem. He had committed to fundamentally changing and expanding who he was, his character. He was tired of thinking that things were fine only to have something come along and upset the balance. He was also tired of not having more ways to respond in various situations. He wanted more overall satisfaction in his life.

Paul's initial bodywork was a jump-start to the usually slow process of revealing character traits and vulnerabilities that is characteristic of long-term analysis. (The therapist does not feel like a stranger for very long once you've done bodywork.)

One of the many ways I worked with Paul on changing his deep prohibition against fighting back was to have him engage his leg muscles by squatting while holding heavy weights. At first, he would chuck the weight down angrily and give up. He did not want to fight to make it happen. He, literally, could not bring himself to do it. It wasn't his style. It wasn't his way. He was fit but not the least interested in engaging his legs in the way I was asking him to.

After many refusals, though, Paul gave in and began screaming as he lifted the weight. He was finally connecting consciously to anger associated with the tension in his legs, anger that came out when he activated those muscles. Immediately following the feeling of anger, Paul had thoughts and memories about terrible, overwhelming experiences with his father.

This led to him re-experiencing the fear and helplessness of those memories and simultaneously discovering a belief holding him back. He realized that a fear of brutal attack by his father (which had happened in the past) kept him from accessing the strength he needed to achieve his aims in the present.

This knowledge, and the integration of his emotions with it, brought Paul to a new place. He had gathered, focused, and released all his strength and power to reach a goal that he had previously avoided and, in the process, he had not been brutally attacked, as he had unconsciously feared. He had faced the fears underneath the anger, integrated them with his newfound understanding, and placed them in the context of his history in a coherent way. This experience and integration changed him dramatically.

In a short time, Paul made some very big changes in the way he related to people. He was not afraid to exert his strength anymore. He pushed for what he wanted out of jobs and was able to stand his ground if he had to. He began to be more assertive in social and work situations and felt much more satisfied and productive as a result.

This story demonstrates a very small part of the overall shift in the way Paul lived and experienced his life. Throughout his long-term commitment to bioenergetic psychoanalysis, he continued to add flexibility to his way of being and, ultimately, gained the emotional satisfaction and peace of mind he wanted.

Stressful emotional situations now merely provide Paul with the opportunity to exercise newly acquired character traits and utilize his well-practiced self-management skills to address a situation rather than allowing a situation to make his life miserable.

He is happy, and he experiences more joy in his life. He is never down in the dumps longer than it takes him to use the tools he learned in therapy to understand what's going on and make the changes necessary to get back to feeling good.

Quite frankly, Paul lives in emotional utopia.

TAILORING THERAPY: WHAT YOU WANT IS WHAT YOU'LL GET

In therapy, you can go as far as you want and be done whenever you feel happy with what you've achieved.

Some clients, like Paul, want to learn and change things about themselves that mystify them: Why do I choose lovers who treat me like crap? Why can't I maintain my emotional stability in the face of certain things? Why do I feel so attached to people? Why can't I let go of people who don't want me as much as I want them? Why am I like this? Why don't I feel happy? Why can't I achieve peace of mind?

For these folks, bioenergetic psychoanalysis is the answer.

Other clients, like Julia, want to deal with one particular issue. I gave her very concrete ways to do that, she ran with them, and that was enough for her. It was the same with James, initially. He needed support to navigate a difficult transition and experienced enough relief through the bodywork to manage on his own. He was very happy with what he got out of the sessions and was ready to take a break.

Committing the time and effort necessary to achieve peace of mind and emotional satisfaction is not for everybody, even if the idea of lasting happiness glimmers at the end of that road. People often break up therapy sessions by months or even years. The support and relief you can obtain in the course of a handful of bioenergetic sessions is invaluable, and I highly recommend them for anyone who is stuck.

As an alternative to private sessions, you could also attend bioenergetic group workshops that last three to five days (see Notes and Resources at the end of the book). However, I do not recommend a group workshop as your first experience in bioenergetics. It could be overwhelming. Test the waters in some individual sessions, and then try a group. There are many international workshops. You could attend them once or twice a year, or even every other year, and benefit greatly from the release of feeling and insight you'd gain in the process.

In workshops, people do bodywork exercises as a group, as well as have individual sessions in front of others. By seeing others work, you realize that your own feelings are normal. You see that others are in the same boat. You will gain a deep feeling of acceptance of yourself through having been a part of a community of people who experience, understand, and accept all feelings in a way that most people do not.

To attain lifelong happiness, peace of mind, and emotional satisfaction, however, you must fundamentally change the way you are. You must, literally, change your brain and completely change the automatic responses you make in the face of stress.

The underlying beliefs you have about yourself that were created in relationships with people who cared for you early on must change. Because of how the brain works, this change can only happen in a consistent and long-term experience that recreates as closely as possible the original circumstances that existed when you formed those beliefs.

This transformation is possible in bioenergetic psychoanalysis.

If it still sounds a bit like magic, it's not. It's science, as you'll see in the next chapter.

CHAPTER 6

The Science of Analysis: Why It Works

Imagine that you follow the same path through the woods outside your house to get to a river, every day. It's well worn and easy to traverse. One day, for whatever reason, your path is inaccessible, so you have to go in a different direction through the woods. It's going to be difficult, and it's going to require a lot more effort than it took to go down the path that's well worn. But if you go down the new path every day, it will become easy and automatic, just as the old one was. The longer the old pathway is left unused, the faster it will get overgrown and finally disappear.

It's the same in your brain. Well-worn pathways in there make up who you are and how you interact with people. The ways you think, feel, and act are based on the firing of your neurons—brain cells—in certain patterns, or pathways. Those pathways were created by your experiences, mostly when you were young.

The more emotionally arousing the situation was when a pathway was created, or the more times the situation was repeated, the more robust the pathway is—and the harder it is to change.

Things as simple as brushing your teeth every day, having a book read to you at night, drinking milk with a peanut butter sandwich, or sitting on the floor to put on your shoes will create strong pathways. Then there are dramatic experiences, the kind that blaze intense pathways immediately.

Imagine a three-year-old who likes to reach for items that are up on the counter, out of his sight. One day, what the boy grasps is the loop of a potholder, which he pulls. On top of it is a boiling hot pot of tea that spills all over him and his Winnie the Pooh footie pajamas, scalding his skin. Telling the boy not to grab things off the counter had not worked, but now he will never forget. He will forever be cautious about the danger of reaching for things he can't see.

The pathway is set and will be very difficult to change. The painful and emotionally arousing experience blazed a pathway instantly.

You must keep this concept in mind if you intend to make any sort of lasting change in your life. The things you are doing and cannot stop yourself from doing, the things you are not doing and want to do but cannot make yourself do, or even your overall state of happiness and peace of mind depend on well-worn pathways. They depend on the patterns in your mind.

It's going to take effort to change those pathways and create new ones.

Let's go back to the new pathway in the woods. If you travel it once, you will probably have to look hard for it the next time, if you can even find it. Only repeated passes are going to make it visible and allow you to find and follow it easily. When you are stressed out, you might forget about the new path and try to use the old one.

In other words, if you want lasting change, you have to commit to frequency and duration. Intense emotional and physical experiences, including bodywork, will help speed up the process.

THE ARCHITECTURE OF THE BRAIN

In our brain the cells are called *neurons*. There is a space between them called a synapse. When they communicate, they are "firing together." With enough repetition or with a lightning bolt of experience, neurons that fire together will "wire together"—hence, the pathways.

Between humans there is something called a social synapse, which is a metaphorical way to describe the space between each of us, similar to the space between our own brain cells. In the same way neurons exchange information across synapses, so it is between humans: each of us affects others, and others us. The social synapse is an important visual for understanding what happens between caregivers[3] and children and in therapy.

Along with understanding the basics of neurons and synapses, it is important for you to know that the brain has a hierarchical system. At its pinnacle is the prefrontal cortex, the part of your brain that makes you human. If the development of your prefrontal cortex has been healthy, "you think well of yourself, you trust others, you regulate your emotions, you maintain positive expectations, and you use your intellectual and emotional intelligence in your moment-to-moment processing."[4]

To envision the relationship of the prefrontal cortex with the rest of your brain, we'll use the simple model developed by Dr. Dan Siegel, a noted neuropsychiatrist. He calls it a "handy model of the brain."

Make a fist, with your thumb turned in and placed underneath all four of your fingers. The area where your wrist and palm meet is your brain stem. It regulates, among other things, your heart rate,

---

[3] Caregivers are parents or anyone who took primary care of you when you were young.

[4] Louis Cozolino, *The Neuroscience of Human Relationship* (New York: W. W. Norton, 2006), 14

breathing, sleeping, and digestion. Your thumb lies over the middle of your palm. The thumb is your limbic system, which controls your emotions. Think of the brain stem and limbic system as your "lower" brain." Your fingers over the top are your cerebral cortex. It is the seat of your "thinking" brain and the "upper" region. The tips of your two middle fingers are your prefrontal cortex, which is your self-conscious regulatory system. It's the part that makes you *you*.

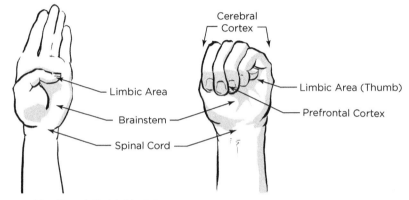

Cerebral Cortex

Limbic Area

Brainstem

Spinal Cord

Limbic Area (Thumb)

Prefrontal Cortex

Dr. Daniel Siegel's Handy Model of the Brain

Notice that the part of your "brain" that makes you *you* touches all the other parts. It is part of your cerebral cortex (your fingers), it touches the limbic system (your thumb), and it touches the brain stem (your palm). The integration of your entire brain happens right there in that prefrontal cortex (the tips of those two middle fingers).

Your brain stem and limbic system were "online" when you were born, but your prefrontal cortex—who you are—was not. It developed in your relationship with your caregivers, starting the day you were born, if not before. The quality of that relationship determined whether it, and therefore you, developed in a healthy or not-as-healthy way. Here's some science jargon to explain it:

The anatomical maturation of the orbitofrontal cortex [the prefrontal cortex, that we're representing by the two fingers] allows for a developmental advance in cognitive and memory functions. The increased functional efficiency that results from such experience-dependent structural development also enables this cortex to generate abstract mental images of faces. Such internal representations encode the infant's physiological-affective responses to the emotionally expressive face of the attachment figure. They can be accessed for regulatory purposes even in the mother's absence.[5]

In other words, when you were "oohed and ahhed" over and your needs were met by your caregiver, your prefrontal cortex developed in a healthy way. You experienced life like this: "I feel such and such a way, and as far as I can tell from experiences with my caregiver, I am okay to feel this."

If nobody made moon eyes at you or attended to you in the way you needed, it was a different story. Your prefrontal cortex would not have developed ideally, and you will have reacted conversely when emotionally aroused. You would have thought, *I am aroused, and when my body feels this way, my experience with my caregiver tells me that I need to not experience this sensation. I need to block it. I need to do whatever is necessary to not feel it.*

In relationship distress, a baby's body automatically begins to block sensation through contraction or spasticity of the muscles or organs. Various parts of the brain remain separate or dis-integrated. The sensory parts (the lower and right brain) do not communicate with the part that "notices" (the prefrontal cortex).

A "good enough" experience with a caregiver provides the foundation of being able to experience consciously and tolerate both negative and positive emotions. An adult with this experience is a happy person who can be conscious of all his emotions. He or she

[5] Allan Schore, *Affect Regulation and the Origin of the Self* (Hillsdale, NJ: Lawrence Erlbaum Associates 1994), 186.

will know that all feelings are healthy and simply provide information for decision making. To elaborate, here is some more science jargon:

> Visual stimulation, embedded in mutual gaze transactions between caregiver and infant, is an essential component of a growth-promoting environment. The mother's emotionally expressive face is the most potent source of visuoaffective information, and in face-to-face inter-actions it serves as a visual imprinting stimulus for the infant's develop-ing nervous system. During visual dialogues the primary caregiver is psychobiologically attuned to the infant's internal state, and in these merger experiences she creates and maintains a mutually regulated symbiotic state in the dyad. In mirroring transactions, a dyadic recipro-cal stimulating system generates an elevation of regulated sympathetic arousal that supports heightened levels of interest-excitement, and enjoyment-joy. This amplification of positive affect is neurochemically mediated by activation of the ventral tegmental dopaminergic system and the stimulation of endogenous opioids in reward centers of the infant's brain. The child's capacity to tolerate higher levels of arousal increases over the first year. These phenomena culminate in very high levels of positive affect at the onset of the practicing phase at the end of the first year.[6]

That is a long and complicated way of saying that a caregiv-er's gaze and the emotional exchanges between caregiver and child develop the brain pathways that must exist for a child to be mentally healthy.

The pathways that develop through interactions with a caregiver allow a child to tolerate increased levels of emotional/physical arousal in a positive way rather than become overwhelmed. By arousal I mean the physical experience of a state of positive emotion, joy, or excitement or the physical experience of distressful feelings such as longing or discomfort.

Emotional arousal is, literally, the body's physical experience of a surge of energy. The energy may be experienced either as positive or negative.

---

[6] Allan Schore, *Affect Regulation and the Origin of the Self* (Hillsdale, NJ: Lawrence Erlbaum Associates 1994), 91.

WHAT THIS MEANS FOR YOU

Research has confirmed it. The quality of the connection between you and your caregivers determined whether you grew to be able to tolerate your emotions and experience them in a positive way or not. This means your emotional struggles, if you have them, definitely began in infancy. Here's why.

The following questions determine the "quality" of the relationship a baby has with its caregiver.

- How does she hold me?
- Does she stare at me with love in her eyes for long gazes?
- How quickly does she meet my needs?
- If I cry, does someone pick me up and comfort me?
- If I am hungry, does someone feed me and enjoy doing it?

A baby's experience of feeling loved depends on having needs like these and many others met, without ambivalence, in a timely manner before undue distress occurs.

If the interactions were "good enough," you learned to experience and manage both positive and negative emotional arousal in a healthy way. You did not get overwhelmed and out-of-sorts easily. Your prefrontal cortex, which was being developed through interactions with your caregiver, was able to put a *brake*[7] on the part of your brain that was aroused. That meant the arousal did not overwhelm you and turn you into a screaming mess, who then may have gotten punished or ignored.

On the contrary, if your interactions with your caregiver were not satisfying, your emotional braking process will be out of whack when you reach adulthood. You'll either feel too much or not at all.

---

[7] Stephen W. Porges, "The Polyvagal Theory: Phylogenetic Substrates of a Social Nervous System," *International Journal of Psychophysiology* 42, no. 2 (Oct. 2001): 123–146.

Fortunately, the brain is "plastic." It is malleable and can change over a lifetime. That means that, later in your life, another person can step in to help you establish or reestablish your ability to self-regulate. That person can provide you with the containing, attuned experience that a caregiver once failed to give you. Anyone can do it for you, but a therapist is specifically trained for that purpose.

Remember Julia, the young lady in college whom I described in chapter 5? Julia had begun worrying about everything before graduation. She had responded by trying to use her will to control herself into not feeling the way she was feeling. That only made her more anxious and unable to handle everyday situations.

In terms of her brain pathways, Julia was caught in limbic, or emotional, functioning. She was unable to engage the rational, regulating part of her brain, the cerebral cortex, to handle what she was feeling. She had "flipped her lid," which is quite an apt description.

As you know from Dr. Siegel's "handy" model, the cerebral cortex is actually on top. When you flip your lid, your cerebral cortex is not engaged and not doing you any good. You cannot regulate yourself.

That is what had happened to Julia. When she came to me, she was on high alert, ready to fight or flee all the time and unable to engage socially. The first thing I did to help her was to bridge the social synapse. I connected emotionally with the feelings she was having: I empathized; I responded verbally and, more important, nonverbally, in ways that made her know I understood her feeling.

The nonverbal process occurs through microfacial movements and something called *mirror neurons*. I also conveyed to Julia my belief that her reaction was normal in the face of the uncertainty in her future. This initial connection provided the foundation for bringing Julia back to functioning in social situations again. She was

MIRROR NEURONS: THE MAGICAL BRAIN CELLS THAT HELP US UNDERSTAND ONE ANOTHER

Everyone has brain cells called **mirror neurons.** These cells fire when you act or move intentionally. They also fire when you see *someone else* make an intentional action or a movement that indicates emotion. The neurons *mirror* the other person even though you have only watched. It's as if you made the action or had the feeling yourself. This firing allows you to know what other people mean or mean to do when they move or how they are feeling, even if they have not "told" you.

It's how the game of charades works. Your friends make movements indicating certain intentions, your mirror neurons fire, and you understand what they are telling you.

It's also how nonverbal communication works between people in regular contexts. A person communicates through eye contact, facial expression, posture, gesture, timing, and volume of speech. When that happens, your mirror neurons fire, indicating to you what was meant in far greater depth than the person could have communicated to you through words alone.

not alone with her feeling anymore.

As mammals, our first line of defense against fearful, overwhelming situations is social engagement. Dr. Stephen Porges, another noted neuropsychology expert, explains this idea in depth in his polyvagal theory. (You can read about it by going to his website at Stephenporges.com.) By connecting with Julia's fear, I helped her reestablish a feeling of safety by providing social engagement. I also helped her put the brakes on her overactive limbic (emotional) system. She was then able to utilize the logic of her cerebral cortex to practice the physical strategies I had taught her. That allowed her to reestablish a connection between her emotional brain and her thinking brain.

INTEGRATING YOUR THINKING AND EMOTIONAL BRAIN

When you were a young child, if your needs were not met or if your caregiver did not or could not satisfy you, for whatever reason, intentional or not, you will be affected. You will live with a sense of not being good, not trusting yourself, and not believing that the world is a good place.

> If your brain's upper, lower, right, and left quadrants are poorly integrated with your prefrontal cortex, understanding what people *really* mean when they communicate will be difficult for you. In fact, unless your brain is well integrated and you are aware of your own feelings, you will never be good at recognizing feelings in others, especially the feelings a person is consciously or unconsciously trying to hide.

As an adult, you will deny the importance of your feelings and the needs you have in your own body. It won't necessarily be extreme, but to some degree, you will have a sense that your needs are not important or your needs are unacceptable. On an unconscious level, you will believe that you have to keep yourself from expressing your needs because they make you bad or unlovable, and/or they are not going to be met anyway.

Research has shown that there are people who say they are not experiencing any feeling at all during an emotionally charged situation. During lab tests, though, they show physiological changes in their bodies exactly like the changes shown in people who are conscious of the emotions in their bodies. These folks are truly not conscious of certain physical sensations.

Most people connect, or associate, feelings in their body with particular emotions, whereas others disconnect, or dissociate, them. Those who dissociate their feelings are not consciously aware of what they are feeling in their body or that they are having an emotion.

They may even see the energy in their bodies as entirely separate from themselves. They do everything they can, unconsciously, to stop the movement of energy through their bodies.

They say, "I'm fine," and they mean it.

When—or *if*—these people come to therapy, they often believe that emotions are "not okay," or are "pointless." They, literally, do not *feel* the way most people do. The conscious part of their brain is not connected to the movement or discharge of energy through their bodies.

Bodywork is often the only way to help these folks reintegrate their dissociated feelings into consciousness.

Here's how that happens. New pathways create links between the cortex (thinking) and the limbic system (emotional feeling). Other new pathways create links between the right brain (the emotional side) and the left brain (the logical side).

When your brain gets integrated through these pathways, you will feel more and better manage what you feel. You will not only tolerate emotions but enjoy varied levels of emotion. And you won't flip your lid, freak out, or feel controlled by something that you do not understand coming from inside you.

Since creating a new you means creating new pathways in your brain, bioenergetic analysis turns out to be especially effective. Putting your body under the stress of bodywork naturally breaks chronic muscular contractions. Feelings—the energy contained in those contractions—get released.

In bioenergetic analysis, you are not having an intellectual experience or insight but, rather, a physical experience that cannot be denied. You are really *doing* something that *makes* you different.

IMPLICIT MEMORY: THE PAST MATTERS

Like it or not, your history is important in most therapies, and bioenergetic psychonalysis is no exception. That's because integrating different types of memories is how we help you get what you want today. Keep in mind that humans have two kinds of memories: *explicit* and *implicit* ones.

Explicit memories are conscious. They are language-based, narrative, and autobiographical memories that you can deliberately call to mind. In other words, they are the stories you tell.

Implicit memories, in contrast, are procedural, sensory, or emotional. You can't think about them, but you have them. They are the demonstration of your unconscious in your attitudes, beliefs, and behaviors.

Walking and serving a tennis ball are implicit memories. Others are your physical or emotional responses to given situations. For instance, your body always reacts a certain way to a set of circumstances even though there does not appear to be any rational link between the two. You get sick every year around your birthday. You get anxious when you have to sit still. You cannot fall asleep unless you have the TV on. They might also be more obvious. You might go on high alert when you are around someone who reminds you of your alcoholic dad. Your body's automatic actions are your implicit memories.

The vast majority of your memories are implicit. They are the ones that shape your current emotional experiences, your self-image, and the quality of your relationships. They are demonstrated even in the micromovements of your body and your muscles. They are impossible to hide.

The more disconnected your implicit and explicit memories are, the greater your experience will be that life is not agreeable, and the more you will want some change that you are unable to effect on your own. In therapy, we merge implicit and explicit memories through bodywork and by analyzing patterns of relationship between you and others. Then we place those merged memories in the context of your history, which gives you a more coherent life story.

People with full, coherent life stories are better at self-regulation. They have more choices about their behavior. They also feel a deeper peace of mind no matter their circumstances.

According to the noted neuropsychologist Dr. Louis Cozolino, there are three forms of implicit memory to address in therapy.[8]

- lack of recall
- superego
- client's expectations of the therapist

A lack of recall, or the absence of memory itself, is a form of memory.

Some people have spotty memories of their childhood. Some people have no memories at all before adolescence. Cozolino says, "A lack of recall strongly suggests high levels of anxiety during childhood that mitigated against the consolidation of long-term memory. It also points to the possibility that dissociative defenses were employed to protect against the dysregulating impact of their earlier circumstances."[9]

People who have vague impressions of childhood as happy or unhappy but do not have a whole lot of explicit memory about it have *split off* (or dissociated) their feelings about it. They may not be able to sleep at night. They may always be on high alert. Their central nervous system is, basically, functioning in a fight-or-flight mode most of the time, and they don't know why.

---

[8] Louis Cozolino, *The Neuroscience of Human Relationship* (New York: W. W. Norton, 2006), 131.
[9] Ibid.

The *superego* is our internal moral police force, the part that tells us whether we are doing right or wrong. It's Jiminy Cricket on our shoulder:

> At a deeper level, the superego is our early implicit memory of our experience of how our parents experienced us. In other words, did our parents seem to cherish, love, and value us? Or did they find us annoying, disgusting, or uninteresting? Our only access to these early experiences is what we see reflected in our self-esteem, the way we treat ourselves and how we allow others to treat us. Brutal self-criticism, overwhelming shame, and a merciless drive for perfection all reflect a harsh and punitive superego, suggesting that at the core of our experience there is an anticipation of abandonment if we do not measure up to expectations. In this situation we are usually completely conscious of how hard we are on ourselves but unaware that our feelings and behaviors are shaped by our implicit memories.[10]

In other words, how hard you are on yourself is *an implicit memory* of your past. If you are hard on yourself, the fact is that your early environment was hard on you, whether you believe it or not.

A client's expectations of the therapist are memories as well: "Our experience of others is created at the interface of our memories of people in our past and our experiences of people in our lives today."[11]

How you react to me in therapy and the way things unfold between us is a blend of both the reality of us together and also your expectations. Your memories of people in your past may trigger ideas of who I am. Sometimes your ideas about me may be distorted based on your history. This is useful to analyze as you strive for happiness.

In therapy, we mainly try to access and work with your implicit memories. As Allan Schore says, "Affect regulation fundamentally underlies and maintains self-function and . . . this process is essentially nonverbal and unconscious."[12] In other words, managing your

---

[10] Louis Cozolino, *The Neuroscience of Human Relationship* (New York: W. W. Norton, 2006), 132.
[11] Ibid, 133.

[12] Allan Schore, *Affect Regulation and the Origin of the Self* (Hillsdale, NJ: Lawrence Erlbaum Associates 1994), 542.

emotions must become an automatic process. If it's not, you will waste valuable energy and ultimately fail.

INTEGRATING MIND AND BODY

I mentioned in chapter 5 that the vagus nerve feeds your brain massive amounts of information from your body. That's why bioenergetics treats the body and mind as one.

As information from all over your body comes into your brain through your vagus nerve, it goes to various areas in the upper, lower, right, and left quadrants. In healthy functioning those quadrants integrate or "wire together." They also integrate with the prefrontal cortex, the part that makes you *you*.

When this happens you will be able to direct conscious awareness to any and all of your feelings, and you will be able to access your unconscious at will. Having this skill means that your sensory information will always be an advantage to you rather than an overwhelming or undermining force.

As your work unfolds in bioenergetic psychoanalysis, you will get better and better at integrating all that unconscious material—those implicit memories—into your consciousness. You will become the master of your emotional universe, unfazed by the attempted manipulations of others, immune to nearly all self-sabotage, and happy no matter your circumstances.

This is emotional utopia.

CHAPTER 7

Structured Therapy or Going It Alone?

I won't deny it: reading self-help books can definitely help you. They can provide insights into why you act the way you do and tell you what actions to take to change. Seminars and retreats by motivational speakers and self-help authors such as Tony Robbins and John Gray are great too. You'll get a major boost from attending them. But how many self-help books are there on your shelves? How quickly does the high from a seminar fade when you return to your busy life?

THE PROBLEM WITH SELF-HELP BOOKS

Even with the best self-help book out there, *The New Psycho-Cybernetics* by Maxwell Maltz and Dan Kennedy, it's too easy to give up on the system it advocates.

Maybe you are not motivated enough, too stressed out, or too busy to focus. What about when it gets uncomfortable? A book cannot help you figure out why you did not begin or continue to work with its system. It can't do that because it does not interface with your unconscious mind and your emotions, which are the real basis for your behavior. Books can only help you with rational, conscious, logical thought processes. They can never provide a way for you to commit to what you say you want.

If it's lasting happiness you're after, a book isn't going to cut it.

You are probably a master at controlling your feelings at most times and in most places. In fact, you are probably so good at it you don't believe there is ever a time for letting out feelings. Maybe you think letting them out will humiliate you or make you look weak in some way. This is a problem if you really want to be happy because you will never be able to fundamentally change that attitude by reading a book.

In addition, you are in control of your emotions when you're reading a book. You can read all you want, but you will go on functioning with the same brain pathways as always unless you put yourself to a test. You will have to be in situations that bring up your best defenses against expressing emotions repeatedly to practice being different. Books are not going to do this for you. Furthermore, doing it outside a therapeutic setting would be ill advised, if not impossible.

Only by *experiencing* your emotions will you ever be able to change your reactions to them and the behaviors they motivate. If you are reading a book, you are in your head. In contrast, bioenergetic psychoanalysis will put you in the crucible of experience that gives you what you need in order to change and become happy.

YOU DON'T HAVE TO *FIGHT* TO WIN

You may be thinking that if you fight hard enough to overcome deeply ingrained motivations, you can achieve happiness on your own. Unfortunately, too many of these motivations are invisible. You don't even know they exist. They are "unknown unknowns." Until they are integrated into your consciousness and experienced in combination with the emotions that power them, you will lose your fight against them again and again.

Some kinds of therapy will help you know why you do what you do. They will help you expose those unknown unknowns.

Other kinds of therapy will help you fortify your resources in the battle of wills against the emotions that fuel the unknowns. That is also what most books help you do.

However, if you are tired of fighting a battle of wills with yourself or you want more change than what "knowing why" can bring you, it might be time to try bioenergetic psychoanalysis. If you do, you won't have to fight for what you want; it will come easily to you.

The irony that you're reading a book about change is not lost on me. Let me use it as an example to explain why therapy would help more than a book ever can.

The next chapter presents some exercises used in bioenergetic analysis that you can try in the privacy of your own home. (These are meant to acquaint you with the process. I'm not suggesting you practice bioenergetic analysis without a therapist.) Among them is one that involves lying on a bed and kicking your feet, pounding your fists, and screaming at the top of your lungs.

This is a very helpful exercise for accessing and discharging feelings. However, there's a good chance you are thinking, *I'm not doing that. That's ridiculous.* And if you let yourself think about why you refuse to do the exercise, you'll probably notice thoughts such as *I'm not a little crybaby,* or even, *I'm not nuts.*

Here's the secret: to get the happiness you want, you have to know that doing the exercises in this book is not crazy and does not mean you are *crazy.* On the contrary, done at an appropriate time and place, these exercises will keep you from being what you fear.

Go ahead and consult any other authorities—any mental-health practitioners—on the definition of crazy. They will tell you that what makes you mentally (and often physically) ill is the inability to experience and integrate all your feelings into consciousness and find appropriate ways to express them. Experiencing, expressing, and integrating your "unacceptable" beliefs and feelings in the presence of an expert you trust is the only way to change your beliefs.

Remember from chapter 6 that you must create new brain pathways to be a new you. Any other method will simply be a willful attempt to make yourself believe something you do not really believe. Since that is what you have been trying up until now, it's not going to bring you a different outcome. Simply reading this book and willing yourself to do the exercises will not help you change the pathways in your brain that say you are crazy.

You need to experience your feelings consciously and analyze your beliefs *in the presence of a trusted authority*. Why? Because, if you do not, you will be missing a key component for gaining lasting peace of mind.

Only a trusted authority who contains, supports, and reflects to you something different from what you already believe will provide you with the raw material you need to eventually embody that trust and authority yourself. This cannot come from a book.

Even in my office, clients often don't want to do bodywork exercises at first because they feel embarrassed. They can *kind* of yell, but they cannot open their throats and literally scream bloody murder. They cannot allow themselves to pound on the foam cube; they stand in front of it and do nothing. It's too embarrassing; they don't "see the point."

Once people allow themselves to do the exercises, they often feel embarrassment or even deep shame. They feel as if there's something wrong with them. They have vocalized or physically expressed a feeling, but they don't know what to do with it. It often makes them feel confused and overwhelmed.

If that happens to you in my office, I help you stay conscious of what you are feeling—whether it is shame, anger, sadness, or rage—and guide you through it. On your own this doesn't happen.

These types of feeling and forcibly controlled energy are holding you back from having what you want in life or are keeping you from quitting what you want to quit doing. Until you understand and believe—until you *know*—that the release of that feeling and energy is wonderful and not terrible, you will be controlled *by* it rather than being *effortlessly* in *control* of it.

I'm not suggesting that you go and express your feelings willy-nilly in the middle of the grocery store. That would be foolish, and you would look crazy. Your feelings are not bad, but there's a time and place to release them.

Think of a child who is repeatedly told, "Don't cry. Be a big boy. Be Mommy's brave little man." That child is not always going to feel brave, but he will have learned that it's not acceptable to be sad or scared, *ever*, so he will not. Only after you *know* (through a repeated and/or intense experience that changes your brain pathways) that releasing feelings is acceptable and good will you come to accept yourself in a way that brings you lasting peace of mind.

COMMIT TO CONNECT

There is an ultimate step you must go through if your goal is to achieve *truly lasting results*. No therapy other than psychoanalysis takes you through it, which is why you will want a practitioner trained in psychoanalysis. This step, one of the most important of all the experiences you will have, is also one of the most difficult to tolerate.

Remember from chapter 2 that you must know, like, respect, and deeply trust your therapist.

Well, there will come a time when a very difficult emotional situation occurs between you two. The reason it happens will be different for everyone. Whatever the details, the end result will be that you feel disappointment, disgust, and anger toward your therapist. You will have to let these feelings well up and spill out toward that very person you now count on to provide support, containment, relief, and a growing belief in the legitimacy of your own experience.

It can cause such intense feelings you don't want to deal with that you'll want to quit. The following email is from an actual patient to show you how this can unfold. Another way is that the client simply walks away with a "good" reason for leaving.

Dear Leah,

I'm writing you this because I'm too chicken to call. I think that I won't be coming back. Whatever is going on right now is too much for me to tolerate, so I'm going to run away. I don't know exactly what is too much to tolerate, but I hated the way I felt today and the way I felt on my way to work. I think it's just better for me to avoid dealing with it, which means I need to stop coming to see you.

I'm surprising myself by doing this. It seems out of character for me, since I don't consider myself a quitter, but for whatever reason, I'm doing it.

Maybe the truth is I just want you to ask me not to leave. Maybe that's my motivation. Maybe in my head, that would prove to me that you really aren't going to forget about me or some other stupid babyish thing like that. Of course, I have also decided that since you are an analyst that you probably won't ask me not to leave, since I suppose that wouldn't be very analytic... Or something along those lines.

Anyway, thanks for everything. I love you.

xo, Jane

Jane didn't end up leaving. Instead, she acknowledged her feelings and worked through the experience *with* her therapist rather than walking away.

Unless you stay, you will never achieve lasting results; there will always be an unaddressed issue. You will always experience intermittent periods characterized by negative emotions you can't understand or quickly shake. They will lead you to make decisions that are detrimental to your personal and business life. Your happiness will not be lasting.

This is one of the most elusive pieces of the puzzle and one of the most important reasons you must *commit* to the process.

Now that you understand why a commitment to bioenergetic psychoanalysis provides you something that self-help or a less committed process does not, I hope you will consider finding someone to help you achieve the lasting happiness you are seeking. There are not a lot of psychotherapists trained in both psychoanalytic and bioenergetic analysis, but I highly recommend that you seek out those who are.

If, after reviewing the list of therapists in the Notes and Resources section, you would like more help finding the right person for you, feel free to contact me. You will find contact information in the About the Author section at the back of the book.

CHAPTER 8

Exercises to Put Bioenergetic Bodywork to Work for You

I n this chapter you will find descriptions of some of the simplest and most powerful bioenergetic exercises, along with instructions on how to do them properly for your benefit.

Don't be surprised if you find that you cannot bring yourself to do many of the exercises at first. They may feel too weird to you. If that's the case, contact a bioenergetic analyst in your area or one listed in the Notes and Resources to guide you through them.

Alternatively, search for Elliott Hulse on YouTube and watch his video "Brain Slave NO MORE!" Hulse is the founder of the wildly popular YouTube health and fitness channel *Strength Camp*. He has created some two thousand videos—and counting. In many of his videos he demonstrates bioenergetic poses and techniques. Seeing a successful, hard-driving entrepreneur like him do these movements might give you the permission you need to let yourself do them as well.

Unlike the bodywork that you might do in bioenergetic analysis, the exercises I describe here for you to try at home are not necessarily going to give you any insight into your feelings. They are a way to discharge energy and let go of some of the chronic tension that can make you feel so terrible.

As you do the exercises, however, you may find that sensations, images, feelings, or thoughts come up. They may be confusing

BODYWORK EXERCISE GUIDELINES

Never do any of these exercises in front of a person you are angry with or to intimidate anyone. Remember there is a time and a place for all emotions and for the expression of all emotions. If you are mad at someone, it is appropriate to release the intense energy of that feeling, but it is not appropriate to do it in front of that person. These exercises are not meant to be done to hurt or intimidate others in any way. They are not for interpersonal communication. They are intended to allow you to release energy so that it does not get trapped in chronic muscular tensions and make you feel miserable.

and make you feel a little overwhelmed. If so, be sure to find someone you trust to talk to about them. And of course, if you become too overwhelmed, contact a mental-health professional right away.

Keep in mind that no matter what you think or feel, there is nothing wrong with you. If you don't know what to do with what has come forth through these exercises, it simply shows that you need to invest in finding a therapist to help you understand your important insight and put it into context.

Many people find the idea of seeking out a therapist intimidating, stupid, or a waste of time and money. However, if thoughts, images, or feelings that you don't understand or that disturb you have come up, it is a good sign that you are going to benefit from professional consultation. You are shaking things loose and becoming aware of what is keeping you from happiness and peace of mind.

You are actually experiencing some of what is inside you, at the core of what is holding you back from everything you want. You have made a breakthrough. You have important information that will be very helpful as you start your journey to happiness.

Even if you don't think anything is bothering you or anything is "wrong" with you, I suggest you try these exercises. I know they can benefit everyone. In fact, I hope that in the future, workplaces will have soundproof rooms where employees can go perform these exercises during the day. An office might have five little studios with mats and foam cubes for people to strike. They would not need to be angry. They might just need a break.

People who spend their days hunched over a computer need to release their chronic tensions. Doing these bodywork exercises for ten minutes a day would make everyone feel much better and even make them more productive. Big corporations have napping and yoga rooms, which is a good thing. Spaces for bodywork exercises would be equally or more helpful.

Finally, be sure not to do these exercises mechanically, as if they are movements you need to *perform.*

If you are slamming your fists on the bed, don't do it for a set amount of time. Instead, do it until you are absolutely exhausted. Or say you've decided to do the adult tantrum exercise every day for two hundred kicks. Don't do two hundred kicks as if you are working through an exercise routine. Make the movements spontaneous. Use a stopwatch at first, and count how long it takes you to do two hundred kicks. If it takes you a minute, then, to allow for spontaneity, set the timer for one minute and kick until the timer goes off, rather than counting kicks.

If you do the exercises that I've described in this chapter whenever you feel you need them, they will provide you great benefit. If you make a habit of doing them on a daily basis, they will benefit you more than you can imagine. You will release built up tensions in your body that you don't even know about, and you will be happier for it. Go ahead. Give it a try.

BREATHING AND GROUNDING

Breathing and grounding exercises are designed to help you slow down, breathe more deeply, and get you "out of your head." There are three poses here:

- basic bioenergetic pose
- breathing stool
- grounding pose

The basic bioenergetic pose brings your focus to your body. The breathing stool and grounding pose are used in a sequence to relax and refresh you.

THE BASIC BIOENERGETIC POSE

First, stand with your feet shoulder-width apart, toes pointing straight forward, heels turned out slightly, knees slightly bent, shoulders relaxed, chest relaxed, and belly relaxed. At the same time, breathe deeply with your mouth slightly open. Notice your body from head to foot (Figure 8.1). Are you vibrating or tingling? Is there tension anywhere? Do you notice any areas where you always hold tension? Do you notice tension in places where you haven't generally felt tension?

Paying attention to your body is a fundamental aspect of bioenergetic analysis. Spend a minute noticing how you feel. Use a timer to make sure you keep focused on your body rather than the time.

Figure 8.1: Basic bioenergetic pose

To intensify the experience, tip your head slightly backward and widen your mouth. Breathe as deeply as you can, as quickly as you can, without making your breath shallow. Do this for about one minute. If you think you are going to pass out, don't worry, you will not. If you get really worried about it, sit, but keep your feet in contact with the ground and keep breathing. Repeat the observations from the first part of this exercise.

THE BREATHING STOOL

Next, you will perform two poses in sequence. The first requires a breathing stool or, if you don't have one, an exercise stability ball. If you don't have an exercise ball, you can even lean over the arm of a couch. You can use a kitchen chair or a barstool with a pillow or rolled-up blanket on top. You can sit on the floor and lean backward over a high pile of pillows, a dense blanket that you have rolled up, or a foam roller. Whatever you use, you will need to be able to bend backward over it (Figure 8.2).

As you lie backward over the exercise ball or whatever you choose, put your arms over your head, and breathe with your mouth wide open. This will stretch the muscles of your chest

Figure 8.2: Breathing stool

and jaw and make you breathe much more deeply. Do this for one minute. If you can't do it for a minute, do it for as long as you can.

You will be energized and invigorated. If you've been feeling depressed or stressed out, you will probably feel much better after relaxing into this stretch, even if it is painful at first.

If you have back problems, be cautious. Do not pass a pain level of seven on a scale of one to ten. Also, be cautious that the exercise ball doesn't roll out from under you when you get up.

GROUNDING POSE

The next pose in the sequence is the grounding pose. After stretching over the breathing stool or equivalent for one minute, move into the bioenergetic grounding pose to relieve your back and let go of any upper body tensions that developed in the back bend.

To get into this pose, stand with your feet shoulder-width apart, toes pointing forward and knees very slightly bent, almost straight but not locked out. Bend forward at the waist, and let your fingertips hang toward the floor. Let your head hang heavily, relax your neck and shoulders, and let your chest and belly soften (Figure 8.3). Keep your weight on the balls of your feet. Breathe deeply into

Figure 8.3: Grounding pose

your belly for one minute. Try to relax your upper body as much as possible, keeping your legs strong and feeling their support as you let go of all the chatter in your head. Focus on the feelings and strength of your legs. That is where the strength of your body primarily resides.

Do the sequence of breathing stool and then grounding pose three times, each exercise for one minute at a time. This will relax and refresh you in a remarkable way.

RELEASING TENSION

The next exercises are designed to help you release pent-up energy. Before you pour a drink or turn on the TV after work, try these exercises. They will bring you instantaneous relief from stress, irritation, and many other negative emotions.

Let's say you get home feeling upset about a meeting. You will be containing this feeling by holding the energy in your muscles, tightening your chest, and constricting your breathing. As a species, we generally hold the stress and tension of anger in the chest, belly, back, and shoulders. When you slam down your arms and vocalize, you release that energy in a focused manner. The tension of the muscles of your chest diminishes, you breathe more deeply, and you benefit by feeling calmer over all.

POUNDING

Stand in front of your bed. Make fists and raise them back over your head, arching your body backward so it makes the shape of an archer's bow. Now slam your fists down on the bed, yelling something like "No!" "Piss off!" or "Get away from me!" if you can, or yell any sound as your fists hit the bed. Be sure to bend your knees slightly so that all the force

Figure 8.4 Pounding

of the movement goes into your fists and your forearms as they slam onto the bed (Figure 8.4).

If you can't yell or verbalize, exhale very strongly. Exhalation activates the "relaxation" part of your nervous system. Repeat this movement until you are exhausted, and you will be surprised how calm you feel.

Alternatively, you can face a bed or couch, take a tennis racket, bend backward in the same manner as described above, and slam the tennis racket onto a pillow or the couch itself. You might go into your backyard and slam a sledgehammer down on a tire or a baseball bat on a pile of sandbags.

However you decide to do the movement, be careful that you are not hitting anything but your intended target. Even if you are feeling out of control, this exercise is advised as long as you are not threatening anyone, hurting yourself or anyone else, or being destructive.

This exercise is extra helpful because as you discharge energy through both physical movement and verbal expression, you release more tension than you would if you were to use one or the other on its own.

ADULT TANTRUM

Another active tension-releasing exercise is what I call the adult tantrum. Clear your bed of all pillows. Lie on your back, making fists. Raise each leg

Figure 8.5 Adult tantrum

straight, not bent, and slam the back of your heels into the mattress one leg at a time, alternating very quickly. As your legs move, add in your arms. Pound your fists on the bed, with your arms straight so that you hit the bed next to your hips (Figure 8.5).

Turn your head back and forth rapidly from side to side, like a child lying on the ground having a temper tantrum. Open your mouth and yell. Wag your tongue around. Kick and yell like this until you are exhausted. It will shake out the chronic muscular tensions all over your body, in your hips, shoulders, neck, and throat. Afterward, you will feel very relaxed.

CONCLUSION

Is Bioenergetic Psychoanalysis for Me?

Do you feel as if you don't have any "problems," but you want to be happy and can't seem to get there? Does your happiness depend on circumstances? Do you want enjoyable relationships and freedom from the emotional manipulation of certain people? If so, then therapy—particularly bioenergetic psychoanalysis—will help you.

During the journey you will get to know yourself in such a way that in most circumstances life throws at you, peace of mind and emotional satisfaction will not elude you for long. You may be thinking you already know yourself and you don't need therapy to help you. However, if you've ever done something you regretted and wondered why on earth you did it, and you truly care to know the answer, then bioenergetic psychoanalysis is for you.

One thing is certain: bioenergetic psychoanalysis is *not* for you if you absolutely do not want to feel your feelings. In fact, if that describes you, don't do *any* bodywork without supervision. It can overwhelm you, and you may never again want to try making your life better.

Therapy can still be helpful to you if you do not want to feel your emotions. You will be better served by cognitive behavioral therapy, which is designed to help you establish and practice willful behavior-change techniques.

Understand, however, that without the frequency and duration of bioenergetic psychoanalysis and without its use of the body and analysis of your relationship patterns, you cannot unlock the emotional satisfaction and peace of mind you seek.

To unlock those things and achieve lasting results, I urge you to find a practitioner of bioenergetic analysis who is also trained in psychoanalysis.

FROM SELF-AWARENESS TO SELF-EXPRESSION TO SELF-POSSESSION

SELF-AWARENESS

According to Dr. Alexander Lowen, the founder of bioenergetic analysis, the first goal of bioenergetic analysis is *self-awareness*. This means being consciously aware of all the feelings in your body.

Scientists call it *interoception*: noticing the feelings in your body in a literal way as tension, tingling, tightness, rigidity, or spasticity (muscle contractions). You need to be able to pay attention to your entire body and notice the feelings throughout. Then you will be self-aware.

This self-awareness leads to what Dr. Bessel van der Kolk calls "agency" in his book *The Body Keeps the Score*. Agency is the technical term for the feeling of being in charge of your life, knowing where you stand, knowing that you have a say in what happens to you, and knowing that you have some ability to shape your circumstances. According to van der Kolk:

Agency starts with what scientists call interoception, our awareness of our subtle, sensory body-based feelings: the greater that awareness, the greater our potential to control our lives. Knowing what we feel is the first step to knowing why we feel that way. If we are aware of the constant changes in our inner and outer environment, we can mobilize to manage them.

SELF-EXPRESSION

When you can tolerate the conscious awareness of *all* your feelings, you are on the road to the second step toward happiness, which is *self-expression*, the ability to express all the feelings inside you. When you can do this by crying, screaming, kicking, hitting, pushing, reaching, whining,

	Known By You	Unknown By You
Known By Others	PUBLIC	BLIND SPOT
Unknown By Others	PRIVATE	UN-KNOWN

What We Know about Ourselves: Levels of Self-Awareness and Goals of Therapy

laughing—whatever it takes to really express all your feelings—you won't waste your energy corralling emotions ever again. You will then have much more energy available to you for productive and enjoyable activities.

SELF-POSSESSION

Finally, once you have become self-aware and self-expressive, your goal is self-possession. *Self-possession* means you are in conscious control of when you express your feelings, even ones you previously kept inside all the time. This is an important goal, since we live in a "civilized" society.

You may be thinking, *I already know when to express my feelings and when not to.* Of course, you do. I'm not talking about learning to control your temper in public or being able to keep from crying in front of other people, though for some people this might be a goal.

What I'm talking about is being willing and able to find times and places where you consciously choose to experience and express feelings you would rather not feel at all, such as longing, weakness, sadness, envy, or hatred. These feelings are a part of the human experience, and to deny their existence is to limit your happiness.

Ridiculous! you think, *Why would I want to feel those types of feeling? Won't I be happier if I feel the good feelings? I'm not really interested in all this feeling-my-feelings stuff.*

If only it were possible to *just* feel the good feelings. To experience life in a happy, positive way; to connect to others in a positive way; to feel joy; and to see, hear, and feel beautiful things, you must feel *all* of your feelings. You cannot pick and choose.

When your body closes off the movement of energy so you can avoid feeling certain feelings, you will not feel anything else, either. Consequently, you can never be truly happy. Besides, isn't it great to listen to your favorite piece of angry or sad music and feel that emotion?

The deeper you go into your pain, the greater heights of joy and ecstasy you will be able to feel when the pendulum swings back in the other direction, and the broader your horizons will be.

Bioenergetic psychoanalysis is a tool, a very powerful one that will help you change the part of you that is keeping you from feeling your feelings. Your unconscious has created a dam that is holding back your feelings, and as I've said, you are not the Hoover Dam. Besides, it's not healthy to hold back your feelings indefinitely.

Granted, you do not want to be a free-flowing river of feelings all the time, either. What you *do* want is to be the floodgate operator. You want to have control over your "flow." You want to be able to crank those floodgates open or closed when you choose. Keeping them slightly open most of the time will give you access to your intuition and gut feelings.

Everybody's journey in analysis is different, depending on the character of the individual. Some people experience a constant feeling of collapsing. In that case, we build you up. Some people cannot manage the intensity of their free-flowing feelings. In that case, we increase your capacity to control your feelings as they flow through you. Others cannot yell, cannot cry, and cannot physically release their emotions, if they feel them at all. In that case, we get you conscious of your emotions and then teach you to express them.

Bioenergetic psychoanalysis will prove to you the legitimacy of consciously experiencing feelings and releasing them in the privacy of your own home, and it will teach you the tools to do it. All the while, you will remain a socially acceptable person. You will no longer lock away any of your feelings so they control your behavior without your choice. Instead, you will conscientiously decide when to express or reveal them. That is self-possession, and it is a pillar of lasting happiness.

If you are hesitant to try bioenergetic psychoanalysis because you know you are not into "feelings," don't worry. It's normal to be apprehensive. If you do therapy, it does not mean you are crazy. And you are not going to go crazy or lose control of yourself. You are not going to become someone else or lose parts of your personality that you like. You will be with a trained guide. You will not be forced to do anything you are not ready to do, and the whole process will be customized to your needs and desires.

If you are ready to unlock lasting peace of mind and to feel more joy in your everyday life, consider bioenergetic psychoanalysis—bio-energetic analysis with a professional trained in psychoanalysis—as your ticket. All you really need to ask yourself is this: *Do I want to put off being happy any longer than I already have?*

ACKNOWLEDGMENTS

First, I'd like to thank Elliott Hulse, the YouTube health and fitness celebrity of Strength Camp, for making me aware of bioenergetics. Without him, I would still be wondering how to accelerate the trip to peak emotional success for my clients.

I'm also deeply thankful to my psychoanalysts, Helena Hjalmarsson and Claudette Krizek. What they gave me is impossible to explain except to say that the changes that occurred in me during my experiences with them are the foundation of my lasting happiness and peace of mind.

To the late Dr. Bob Glazer, thank you for bringing Alexander Lowen's bioenergetic analysis to Florida. To my trainers, Scott Winfield, Ana Zebel, John Yong, Laurie Ure, Silvina Henriquez, Ana Murillo, Alberto Wang, Marzena Barszcz, Susan Kanor, Bill O'Donnell, Len Carlino, Diane Gobrogge, Soledad Valenzuela, and Ron and Gloria Robbins: your patience, love, and skill guided me through the ups and downs that come with bioenergetic analysis training, added much to my foundation of happiness and peace of mind, and made me the bioenergetic practitioner I am today. Thank you.

I'd also like to extend many thanks to the late Dr. Aracelia Pearson-Brok, my Columbia professor, and her husband, Dr. Albert Brok, who introduced me to the world of psychoanalysis and helped me see the beginning of the path to my life's work.

This book was a challenge. I appreciate the assistance and creativity from my photo team, Bob Sargent of Sargent Photography, Chris Wescott, Yvette Moreno, and Laurie Eichar; my readers and editors,

Sabine O'Laughlin, Kate Donaho, Tom Schneider, and Sonia Davis; and the team at Advantage. Finally, my deepest gratitude goes to Koré MacKenzie, without whom I could not have written this book.

ABOUT THE AUTHOR

Leah Benson is a licensed psychotherapist in the Tampa Bay Area. Leah received bachelor's degrees from the University of Texas at Austin in 1994 and subsequently worked with children in both recreational and therapeutic settings. In 1999 she moved to New York City to attend Columbia University, where she earned both an EdM and an MA degree in counseling psychology. During her graduate studies, she worked with adults, adolescents, and children in psychiatric hospital and outpatient settings, helping them overcome a broad range of personal, relationship, and work challenges.

Before training in bioenergetic analysis, Leah studied psychoanalytic theories, concepts, and methods, including Freudian psychoanalysis, character analysis, object relations theory, self-psychology, relational and intersubjective theories, and ego psychology. She also studied and was certified in neurolinguistic processing. She has a strong interest in neuropsychology and structural changes that occur in the brain due to therapy.

Leah's personal journey through psychotherapy includes ten years of psychoanalysis and ongoing experience in bioenergetic therapy in workshops, personal sessions, and training. She participates in approximately two hundred hours of continuing education each year.

Leah's ongoing work as a therapist and client has enabled her to empower others with knowledge and skills to achieve emotional satisfaction and a happy life. This is what she wants, more than anything else, to pass on to others. It is the focus of her exceptional and exclusive practice.

301 W. Platt St., Tampa, FL 33606

Info@EmotionalUtopia.com

Phone: (813) 452-0111

Fax: (727) 845-4176

Notes and Resources

Finding a Therapist

If you'd like to find a therapist via the Internet, search:

- bioenergetic analysis;
- body-oriented psychotherapy; or
- relational somatic psychotherapy.

It's really important to find a therapist who has been trained in and understands body-mind therapy work. If you want lasting results, seek a practitioner who has also been trained extensively in psychoanalysis. Better yet, choose one who has had psychoanalysis and can tell you he/she is, without reservation, happy, peaceful, and emotionally satisfied.

A warning: the first things that may come up in a search engine are people who offer bioenergetic medicine, bioenergetic feedback, energy field therapy, or detoxification of bioenergetic imbalances. These are *not* the same thing as bioenergetic analysis. Any system that involves things such as "the manipulation of bioenergetic fluxes to positively affect health" is not what this book has been describing.

When you are investigating practitioners, keep in mind that some psychotherapists are flexible about whether or not they include bodywork. (I am one of these therapists.) Others limit themselves to either bioenergetic analysis or traditional talk therapy. Find a psychoanalyst who specializes in bioenergetic analysis, and consult with that specialist. See what that person feels like to you. This is the most important part of choosing any therapist. Research has consistently shown that *the* most important aspect of therapy that changes people in a positive way is the relationship between client and therapist.

If you live in or near an urban center, you may be fortunate enough to have a choice of therapists. If you do not live near a major population center, you may have to make a bigger investment of time, energy, and money to find and meet with a bioenergetic analyst. You may have to regularly fly to see someone out of your area. Remember this is an investment in yourself, like any other mastery you seek.

There are also practitioners who offer short-term, intensive, bioenergetics sessions, usually between three and seven days. You can arrange the details of these sessions by phone. You can also attend bioenergetics workshops, some of which are available for people who have never done any bodywork.

Where to Find Bioenergetic Analysts and Information about Bioenergetics Workshops

The Florida Society for Bioenergetic Analysis
http://www.bioenergetics-society.com/

The International Institute for Bioenergetic Analysis
http://www.bioenergetic-therapy.com/index.php/en/

The Alexander Lowen Foundation
http://www.alexanderlowenfoundation.com/links_new3.html

PRACTITIONERS WHO PROVIDE MULTIDAY INTENSIVES

Leonard Carlino, PhD

100 Evergreen Ave.

Philadelphia, PA 19118

(215) 242-3232

Pam Chubbuck, PhD

info@VitallyAlive.com

Vitally Alive Core South

8733 Lake Drive

Snellville, GA 30039

(770) 388-0086

Diane Gobrogge, DOM, LAc

dianegobrogge@gmail.com

108 North Kerr Ave. Ste D6

Wilmington, NC 28405

(910) 350-2740

Robert Lewis, MD

docboblewis@gmail.com

155 E. 91st St. Ste 1B

New York, NY 10128

(212) 427-3556

PRACTITIONERS WHO COMBINE BIOENERGETIC ANALYSIS AND PSYCHOANALYSIS

Marzena Barszcz, MA

kontakt@marzenabarszcz.com

Warsaw, Poland

+48 605–851–807

Grzegorz Byczek, CBT

Warsaw, Poland

grzegorzbyczek.com

John Conger, PhD

303 Arlington Ave. B4

Kensington, CA 94707

(510) 962-4061

Christine J. Harris, MS, LMFT, CBT

therapy@harris4.com

11 W. Dry Creek Circle, Ste. 140

Littleton, CO 80120

(303) 794-7761

www.cjoyharris.com

Viviane Hens

viviane@bttvh.com

3434 Shallowford Rd. Ste. H-6B

Marietta, GA 30062

(678) 908-6219

www.bttvh.com

Robert Hilton, PhD
150 Paularino #185
Costa Mesa, CA 92626
(714) 850-9905

Charles Martin, PhD, licensed psychologist
Gainesville, FL
(352) 375-7756
www.drcharlesmartin.com

Peggy S. Wegener, LMHC
2950 Halcyon Lane, Ste. 204
Jacksonville, FL 32223
(904) 252-1900

Scott Winfield, LCSW
31 SE 11th St.
Fort Lauderdale, FL 33316
(954) 527-2664

LEARNING THROUGH YOUTUBE VIDEOS

In the following videos you will find excellent, simple explanations of many of the scientific concepts that underpin the bioenergetic psychoanalysis method. These videos will help you understand that process more deeply.

Dan Siegel, MD

"On How You Can Change Your Brain"

Dr. Siegel explains that you can rewire your brain and how doing so changes how you relate to yourself and others.

"On Integrating the Two Hemispheres of Our Brains"

Dr. Siegel explains how integration of your brain makes you more balanced and compassionate.

"On Integration as a Source of Strength"

Dr. Siegel explains the good things that will happen in your life if you engage in a process that increases your self-awareness. He calls it mindsight; I call it bioenergetic psychoanalysis.

"Brain Hand Model: Empathy and Cognition"

Dr. Siegel explains his "handy model of the brain."

"'Being' versus 'Doing'"

Dr. Siegel explains how focusing on your physical experiences helps you develop kindness toward yourself.

"'Flipping Your Lid': A Scientific Explanation"

Dr. Siegel explains how the prefrontal cortex helps you regulate yourself and the idea that development of this part of your brain happens in a relationship.

"On Recreating Our Past in the Present"

Dr. Siegel explains the "pathways" in your brain and how you can change them through therapy.

"On the Idealization of Parents"

Dr. Siegel explains how avoiding the reality of parental faults hampers your ability to grow.

"On Emotional Balance"

Dr. Siegel explains that your ability to tune in to yourself and others and to regulate your body and your emotions comes from having had someone "attune" to you.

"Mirror Neurons: 'The Discovery'"

Dr. Siegel explains mirror neurons.

"TEDxBlue – Daniel J. Siegel, MD – 10/18/09"

This longer video contains most of the information in Dr. Siegel's shorter videos above. Dr. Siegel explains that relationships are our life's blood and the brain is the social organ of our body.

Stephen W. Porges, PhD

"The Polyvagal Theory: Neuropsychological Foundations"

Dr. Porges talks briefly about the vagus nerve and how being in an attuned relationship promotes physiological well-being.

Elliott Hulse

"Brain Slave NO MORE!"

Elliott Hulse demonstrates many of the expressive or tension-releasing bioenergetic movements and talks about the development of chronic muscular contraction and its correlation to unhappiness.

AUDIO RECORDINGS

Robert Hilton, PhD

"Relational Somatic Psychotherapy"

This is a recorded interview of the longtime bioenergetic analyst and bioenergetic trainer Dr. Robert Hilton, who explains the deficit in most bioenergetic therapies resulting from the lack of focus on the relationship between client and analyst.

BOOKS

The New Psycho-Cybernetics **by Maxwell Maltz and Dan Kennedy**

This wonderful self-help book is one of the most systematic and plain-spoken offerings on the idea of the unconscious and how to work with it yourself. It was written in the 1960s by Maxwell Maltz and updated in 2000 by marketing guru Dan Kennedy. The book presents an excellent explanation of the development of the unconscious and how it affects your daily life. It is written in nonacademic language and is a practical guide to instructing your unconscious to direct your life in any way you choose.

Mindsight: The New Science of Personal Transformation **by Dan Siegel, MD**

Many obstacles to a full life, from everyday stress to severe trauma, can be overcome by developing what Dr. Siegel calls mindsight. Mindsight is our ability to perceive the mind and literally redirect the flow of energy and information within our brain. Through this powerful capacity for insight and empathy, we can "rewire" crucial connections, create dynamic linkages, and open ourselves to relationships in a new way.

Why Therapy Works **by Louis Cozolino, PhD**

Dr. Cozolino explains why therapy works and why it matters that we understand how it works.

Authentic Happiness **by Martin Seligman, PhD**

Dr. Martin Seligman says that happiness is not the result of good genes or luck. He says real, lasting happiness comes from focusing on one's personal strengths rather than weaknesses—and working with them to improve all aspects of one's life. Using practical exercises, brief tests, and a dynamic website program, Seligman shows readers how to identify their highest virtues and use them in ways they haven't yet considered.

References

Beebe, Beatrice et al. "The Origins of 12-Month Attachment: A Microanalysis of 4-Month Mother-Infant Interaction." *Attachment & Human Development* 12 (2010): 3–141. doi:10.1080/14616730903338985.

Carlino, Leonard, PhD. Personal communication. November 2015.

Cozolino, Louis. *The Neuroscience of Human Relationships.* New York: W. W. Norton, 2006.

Luft, Joseph, PhD and Ingham, Harrington, PhD. *The Johari Window.* 1955.

Porges, Stephen W. "The Polyvagal Theory: Phylogenetic Substrates of a Social Nervous System." *International Journal of Psychophysiology* 42 (2001): 123–146.

Schore, Allan. *Affect Regulation and the Origin of the Self.* Hillsdale, NJ: Lawrence Erlbaum Associates.

Siegel, Dan, MD and Tina Payne Bryson, PhD. *The Whole Brain Child.* New York: Bantam Books Trade Paperbacks, 2012.

van der Kolk, Bessel. *The Body Keeps the Score.* New York: Penguin, 2014.

CPSIA information can be obtained
at www.ICGtesting.com
Printed in the USA
BVOW07s2041290916

463572BV00044B/93/P

9 781599 326856